2nd edition
Fully revised
and extended

Understanding and Responding to Behaviour that Challenges in Intellectual Disabilities (2nd edition)

A handbook for those that provide support

Edited by Peter Baker and Tony Osgood

TIZARD
University of Kent

Challenging
BEHAVIOUR
foundation

Pavilion

Understanding and Responding to Behaviour that Challenges in Intellectual Disabilities (2nd edition)

A handbook for those who provide support

© Pavilion Publishing & Media Ltd

Published by:
Pavilion Publishing and Media Ltd
Blue Sky Offices
Cecil Pashley Way
Shoreham by Sea
West Sussex
BN43 5FF

Tel: 01273 434 943
Email: info@pavpub.com

Published 2019

A catalogue record for this book is available from the British Library.

ISBN: 978-1-911028-95-6

Pavilion Publishing and Media is a leading publisher of books, training materials and digital content in mental health, social care and allied fields. Pavilion and its imprints offer must-have knowledge and innovative learning solutions underpinned by sound research and professional values.

Editors: Peter Baker and Tony Osgood
Cover design: Emma Dawe, Pavilion Publishing and Media Ltd.
Page layout and typesetting: Emma Dawe, Pavilion Publishing and Media Ltd.
Printing: CMP Digital Print Solutions

Contents

About the authors

Dr Peter Baker (editor)
Dr Peter Baker (BCBA-D) is a Senior Lecturer in Intellectual Disability at the Tizard Centre, University of Kent. He worked as a Consultant Clinical Psychologist for the NHS in Sussex for over 20 years where he had leadership responsibilities for learning disability psychology services in East Sussex and Brighton & Hove. He lectures at the Tizard Centre on certificate, diploma, graduate and masters programmes and is widely published in the area of challenging behaviour and intellectual disability. He is the senior editor of the *International Journal of Positive Behaviour Support*.

Dr Julie Beadle-Brown
Julie Beadle-Brown is Professor in Intellectual and Developmental Disability at the Tizard Centre, University of Kent and in Disability Studies at La Trobe University in Melbourne. Her teaching, research and consultancy focuses on promoting better quality of life for people with learning disabilities and autism through high quality, community-based services at both national and international levels. In particular, she has researched, published and consulted on deinstitutionalisation and community living and on person-centred approaches such as active support, and what is needed in terms of workforce development and leadership to ensure better quality of life outcomes for people with disabilities.

Dr Jill Bradshaw
Jill Bradshaw is a Senior Lecturer in Intellectual and Developmental Disabilities at the Tizard Centre. She is also a Speech and Language Therapist. Jill is Director of Studies for the undergraduate programmes at Tizard and also manages the centre's consultancy work. She has over 25 years of experience of working with people with intellectual and developmental disabilities and their families.

Dr Shelley Brady
Shelley Brady is an award winning BCBA-D in the areas of research and innovative practice. She has worked in the area of intellectual disability, autism spectrum condition and education since 2002. Throughout that time she has been a tutor, supervisor, consultant and lecturer across a wide range of settings and services. Shelley is currently working in the disability services in the Institute of Technology, Co. Sligo, supporting 3rd level students. She is passionate about creating an inclusive society where education, skills development and employment are accessible to all.

Viv Cooper

Viv is the parent of a young man with severe learning disabilities who displays a range of behaviours described as challenging, some of which are life-threatening. In 1997 Viv founded the Challenging Behaviour Foundation (CBF), a small national charity providing information and support to professionals and families caring for individuals with severe learning disabilities and behaviour described as challenging (www.challengingbehaviour.org.uk). Viv participates in groups and networks at local, regional and national level. The CBF established the Challenging Behaviour – National Strategy Group which Viv chairs. Viv was awarded an OBE for services to families and people with severe learning disabilities.

Professor Shoumitro (Shoumi) Deb

Shoumitro (Shoumi) Deb, MBBS, FRCPsych, MD (s.deb@imperial.ac.uk) developed the International and the National Guidelines on the use of psychotropic medication among adults with intellectual disabilities (ID) (www.ld-medication.bham.ac.uk). He led the development of the first ever European guide for the diagnosis of mental disorders among adults with ID (www.eamhid.org). He developed a screening instrument for dementia in people with ID which has been translated into more than 12 languages for worldwide use. He has over 220 publications and has done over 220 conference presentations nationally and internationally, and was a member of the WHO ICD-11 work group on ID.

Roy Deveau

After undertaking various nursing roles Roy established a small residential care service in 1987 for people with ID who at times showed behaviour described as severely challenging. In 2004 Roy made a career move to research at the Tizard Centre, undertaking research focused upon practice leadership and supporting staff to work positively with people who may challenge them at times. Having published several articles and undertaken consultancy in reducing restrictive practices and practice leadership, Roy is approaching retirement, which never seems to happen. Roy recently co-wrote a book on reducing restrictive practices with Sarah Leitch, published by BILD.

Professor Rachel Forrester-Jones

Rachel is Professor of Social Policy at the University of Bath and Hon. Professor of Social Inclusion at the University of Kent where she held the role of Director of the Tizard Centre until 2018. Her research spans the life course of people with learning disabilities, especially in relation to social networks and social support. As a qualified Barrister (NR), Rachel also has a special interest in the law in relation to the lives of people with learning disabilities and she is a member of a legal panel which seeks to improve people with learning disabilities' access to legal advice.

Isabelle Garnett

Isabelle is the mum of two extraordinary young people, one of whom has autism and a learning disability. She has decades of experience in navigating the labyrinth of education, social care and health services, most recently fighting to get her son out of an acute treatment unit and to have a positive and fulfilling life in the community. Isabelle is an Expert by Experience Advisor on NHS England's Children and Young People's STOMP STAMP (Stop the Over-Medication of People with learning disabilities, autism or both) campaign as well as its National CYP Transforming Care Programme.

Dr Nick Gore

Nick Core is a Clinical Psychologist and Senior Lecturer/Researcher in Learning Disability based at Tizard Centre, University of Kent. He has a special interest in positive behavioural support, early intervention, emotional well-being and partnership working with families and staff teams. Nick has written several conceptual accounts relating to these areas, developed a range of intervention approaches and conducted research to further the evidence base. He has helped establish a variety of multi-stakeholder networks and initiatives in the field that aim to facilitate good practice and positive outcomes for people with disabilities and those who support them.

Dr Maria Hurman

Maria Hurman has a Learning Disability Nursing role with the Children and Young People's Learning Disability Team across Surrey and is an Honorary Lecturer at The Tizard Centre, University of Kent. Maria offers advice and support to families and schools which involves carrying a caseload of young people who experience mental ill health or present behaviour described as challenging. Maria's interests include functional assessment, positive behaviour support, teaching others, Transforming Care, rapport between people with intellectual disabilities and paid or family carers and functional communication. Maria has completed a PhD at the Tizard Centre with the focus on rapport.

Dr Edwin Jones

Edwin Jones, Service Improvement and Research Lead at Swansea Bay University Health Board holds honorary posts at the University of South Wales and International University of Catalonia. He leads three accredited e-learning qualifications in PBS, is a member of the BILD Professional Council, the PBS academy, Restraint Reduction Network and SF Darrin PBS research network and an editorial board member of several journals. Edwin chairs the All Wales Challenging Behaviour Community of Practice and sits on the Welsh Government Learning Disability Ministerial Advisory Group. His main interests include positive behavioural support, challenging behaviour, active support and practice leadership.

Dr Anne MacDonald

Anne MacDonald is a Senior Research Fellow at the Institute of Health and Wellbeing at the University of Glasgow, where her role is to lead on research in relation to people with intellectual disabilities and behaviours that challenge. She has worked within social care service provision for the past 25 years, with a particular focus on managing the implementation of positive behavioural support. Anne is also seconded part time to the Scottish Government, where she leads a project in relation to out-of-area placements and delayed discharge from hospital for people with intellectual disabilities and complex needs.

Dr Jonathan Mason

Jonathan Mason is Associate Professor of Clinical Psychology at the University of the Sunshine Coast in Queensland, Australia. Prior to completing his training in clinical psychology, he completed a PhD in the Applied Psychology of Intellectual Disability, and has published widely in the areas of assessment and treatment of mental health and behavioural problems in people with intellectual disabilities. His favourite colour is red (the fastest colour).

Stephen C. Oathamshaw

Stephen Oathamshaw is Consultant Clinical Psychologist and Head of Specialty for the Clinical Psychology Service at the Scottish Borders Learning Disability Service. Stephen started working with people with learning disabilities in 1988. He trained as a learning disability nurse qualifying in 1993, and worked for a number of years with people who challenge services in residential services and specialist challenging needs community teams in South London. Stephen re-trained as a Clinical Psychologist qualifying from the Manchester training course in 2004. During his psychology training Stephen developed interests in adapting cognitive behavioural therapy for people with learning disability and in psychological therapy for people with learning disabilities and psychosis, interests he has continued to develop through clinical work, research and publications.

Tony Osgood (editor)

Tony Osgood is a Senior Lecturer in Intellectual Disabilities at the Tizard Centre, University of Kent. He teaches on positive behaviour support, autism, intellectual disabilities, human services and challenging behaviour. He has a background in direct support work in the NHS and the private and voluntary sector. He is interested in service organisations, person-centred support, family support, inclusion, diversity, mindfulness and communities of practice. He has taught and lectured in the UK and Europe and has written extensively on a variety of topics. His first book on challenging behaviour, *Supporting Positive Behaviour in Intellectual Disabilities & Autism: Practical Strategies for Working with Challenging Behaviour* is to be published in 2019.

Dr Ciara Padden

Ciara Padden, BCBA-D is a lecturer in learning disability at the Tizard Centre, University of Kent. She oversees postgraduate programmes in Applied Behaviour Analysis and Positive Behaviour Support, and engages in related research and consultancy. She is currently on the board of directors for the UK Society of Behaviour Analysis, and co-chairs the Adult Skills Development research group of the Sharland Foundation Developmental Disabilities ABA Research and Impact Network. She is passionate about ensuring high quality support for people with disabilities and their carers, with a particular interest in using behavioural approaches to develop skills, increase independence and enhance quality of life.

Dr Lawrence Patterson

Lawrence Patterson is a qualified Clinical Psychologist with 15 years' experience working in the NHS with people with learning disability and autism. He currently works in Portsmouth Integrated Learning Disability Service with Solent NHS Trust. Lawrence also has a brother with severe learning disability who has been described as sometimes displaying behaviour that challenges. He has research and clinical interests in involving carers and family members in improving the quality of care and support for people.

John Shephard

John Shephard has worked with people with learning disabilities throughout his career and since 1992, after studying at the Tizard Centre, has specialised in promoting effective support for those who present behaviours that challenge. He spent over twenty years working with an NHS psychology department in East Sussex as part of a specialist behavioural support team, providing assessment, consultancy and training to the local community, promoting approaches based on positive behavioural support. He continues to teach positive behavioural support as an independent consultant.

Jenna Szymanski

Jenna Szymanski is a Learning Disability Nurse. Jenna trained at the University of Southampton and qualified in 2008. Since then Jenna's nursing career has been focused around supporting individuals who present with behaviour that challenges. Jenna has worked at a residential setting for adults with learning disabilities, an inpatient assessment and treatment service for adults with learning disabilities who present with behaviour that challenges, as a Community Learning Disability Nurse and she is currently working in an Intensive Support Team. In 2016, Jenna completed a post graduate diploma in Applied Behaviour Analysis at the Tizard Centre.

Professor Sandy Toogood

Sandy Toogood is Head of Clinical Services at Abbey School for exceptional children and Honorary Professor in the College of Humans Sciences at Bangor University. Sandy contributed to the original development of active support and was a member of the first specialist behavioural support service in the UK working out from the University of Kent. He has researched, published, trained and taught extensively on behaviour analysis, positive behavioural support, and active support. Sandy was a founding member of the PBS Academy, an advisor at BILD's Centre for the Advancement of PBS, and is currently Associate Editor of the *International Journal of Positive Behavioural Support*.

Holly Young

Holly has a background in psychology, with an MSc in Health Psychology. She has many years' experience of helpline work and runs the Family Support Service at the Challenging Behaviour Foundation in her role as Family Support Lead. She has provided specialist information and support around challenging behaviour to families and professionals at the CBF for over eight years. She has written and reviewed information resources for the Challenging Behaviour Foundation and contributed to joint resources with other organisations, such as BILD, Skills for Care, Housing Options and Mencap. Holly has also spoken at conferences and given presentations to students. Holly has a particular interest in human rights and improving partnership working for the benefit of people with learning disabilities.

Foreword: Responding to a changing world

By Peter Baker & Tony Osgood

Since the last edition of this book titled *Challenging Behaviour and People with Intellectual Disabilities* was published in 2011, a great deal has changed in the world of services for people with intellectual disability who present behaviour that challenges.

Prior to 2011, a quiet evolution of best practice in supporting people was taking place, and the term positive behaviour support was increasingly heard. In practice this meant different things to different people, but broadly it implied behaviour that challenges was to be understood as carrying a message. Through understanding this message, support could be tailored to better meet a person's needs. Positive behaviour support requires us to change the manner in which we support people, and importantly, change how we think about behaviour that challenges.

Since 2011 there has been significant growth in positive behaviour support (PBS). We have seen the development of the PBS Academy and its definition of competency standards becoming increasingly relevant. The Academy has helpfully set out what PBS looks like in practice. Significantly, in 2011 the need for the wider implementation of the values and practices of PBS was highlighted by the horrific events at Winterbourne View. This private hospital was the subject of a BBC undercover investigation showing emotional and physical abuse. Not only were individuals held responsible for the ill-treatment of vulnerable people at Winterbourne View, the systemic failures of methods of keeping people safe were highlighted. A national debate began concerning the suitability of hospitals in supporting people with intellectual disabilities.

Central government was quick to respond and initiated the *Transforming Care* programme. This was formally launched in 2012. It recognised that what happened in Winterbourne View was not a case of 'bad apples' but a wider and fundamentally more dangerous 'bad barrel'. Winterbourne View was merely the tip of an iceberg – an iceberg that had in fact been previously represented on the cover of the Mansell reports of 1993 and 2007 (Department of Health 1993; 2007).

Transforming Care stated that reviews undertaken in the wake of the Winterbourne scandal had revealed a 'widespread failure to design, commission and provide services which give people the support that they need close to home, and which are in line with established best practice. Equally, there was a failure to assess the quality of care outcomes being delivered for the very high cost of placements at Winterbourne View and other hospitals' (Department of Health, 2012). It made the powerful statement that 'we should no more tolerate people with learning disabilities or autism being given the wrong care than we would the wrong treatment being given for cancer'.

The policy rightly identified one of the problems being the model of provision which involves taking people far away from their homes, families and loved ones, and placing them in large 'assessment' or 'hospital' facilities which struggle or fail with their sole purpose, that of assessing, understanding and treating people. The multi-agency solution was to review all hospital placements, focus on reducing the numbers of people in such facilities and increase the inspection and regulation of these places. Alongside these recommendations came specific endorsement of PBS.

Since that time *Transforming Care* has failed to meet its objectives. It unfortunately remains the case that large numbers of people with intellectual disability and/or autism are still placed in hospital care some distance from their homes and that, while in such placements, many will experience high-risk physical interventions, contrary to current policy guidance. The people living in such places will experience the risk of assault from others. Dave Allen, in a recent critique of the policy, concluded:

'The inappropriate use of inpatient facilities for this group stems in the first place from a fundamental lack of competence to meet needs at a local level. Failing strategically and systematically to develop such competence fails to address the principal reason for admissions to such services. Unfortunately, though the policy did flag this as an objective, the main focus of Transforming Care has been closing hospital beds. To use a crude analogy, rather than turning off the taps, attention has been focused on emptying the bath. The revolving pattern of admissions described above is an inevitable consequence.'
(Allen, 2018)

This brings us to the purpose of this handbook. It could be argued that the remaining legacy of *Transforming Care* has been to highlight, endorse and increase awareness of the importance of PBS as a framework for designing services for people with intellectual disabilities in order to avoid or manage behaviour that challenges. Our intention then has been to produce summaries of different aspects of the PBS framework that are both accessible and practical.

The handbook is written for those people who work or live directly with people with intellectual disabilities who present behaviour that challenges. Throughout the book, in keeping with current consensus, we have used the term 'behaviour that challenges'. We have taken a 'reference lite' approach to make the content speak for itself. Our intention is that the book will be life changing

– in as much as the lives of people with intellectual disabilities will change for the better as a result of people who are important to them, namely family members and support staff reading it, and more importantly, changing how they understand people and behaviour as a result.

The editor's royalties from this book go to The Challenging Behaviour Foundation (CBF). The CBF has for many years provided a voice for parents supporting children whose behaviour challenges those around them. The CBF are advocates for person-centred support and the implementation of research and policy. Their work has proven a lifeline for parents as well as a perspective many policy makers and service providers have benefitted from hearing. We are pleased this book will contribute to supporting the work of CBF.

References

Allen D (2018) Transforming Care: a case study in failure. *International Journal of Positive Behavioural Support* **8**(2) 4-8.

Department of Health (1993) *Services for People with Learning Disabilities and Challenging Behaviour or Mental Health Needs* (The Mansell Report).

Department of Health (2007) *Services for People with Learning Disabilities and Challenging Behaviour or Mental Health Needs* (The Mansell Report) (revised edition) [online]. Available at: https://www.kent.ac.uk/tizard/research/research_projects/dh2007mansellreport.pdf (accessed February 2019).

Department of Health (2012) *Transforming Care: A national response to Winterbourne View Hospital*. London: DH publishing.

Part 1:
Clearer Values

The book is split into four sections, each representing a crucial step in understanding behaviour that challenges.

Children and adults with intellectual or developmental disabilities (IDD) and/or autism who display behaviour that challenges those around them, continue to be particularly vulnerable to being misunderstood and inappropriately supported, despite policy and best practice guidance.

How we support children and adults with IDD and/or autism depends in part on how we think about them and the behaviour that challenges. The reality is children and adults whose behaviour challenges those around them are vulnerable to having fewer opportunities to engage in society, having their quality of life reduced, experiencing abusive or coercive practice, and being placed in schools or services many miles from home. Many families of children whose behaviour challenges often remain likewise unheard and isolated.

The first section contains five chapters, each presenting fundamental approaches to thinking about and responding to behaviour that challenges. These chapters set out current understanding of what behaviour that challenges is, the legal contexts, and the values of good support.

Chapter 1: What is behaviour that challenges?

By Edwin Jones

Summary

Behaviour can be considered challenging when other people think it is socially unacceptable, difficult or dangerous. It increases the likelihood that the person will be rejected, have a poor quality of life and be treated badly. This social definition can include a wide range of behaviours, such as shouting, threatening, hurting other people, hurting yourself, destroying things and so on. These behaviours happen for various reasons and are reactions to the person's environment. They can be a way to communicate, to get or avoid things. Everyone is different, so to understand the reasons *why* someone behaves in a particular way we have to take a person-centred approach. We use the term 'challenging' because we know it is possible, but not always easy, to understand the reasons why and then improve environments so the person is supported to have good quality of life and get what they need, without having to behave in challenging ways.

Behaviour that challenges or the older term 'challenging behaviour' is not a medical diagnosis in the same way as, for example, measles or salmonella are specific diseases, caused by a virus or bacteria inside the person. Behaviour that challenges should not be used to label and blame the person, or imply that everyone who may behave in challenging ways are the same. This chapter explains the correct meaning of 'behaviours that challenge', and why when properly understood it is the foundation for the good practice described throughout this book.

'Behaviour that challenges': what's in a name?

Intellectually disabled people who behave in ways that other people find challenging are one of the most disadvantaged groups in society. The words we use have the power to harm or help vulnerable people because they influence attitudes. Discrimination was more prevalent only a few decades ago when racist, sexist or homophobic language and attitudes were common. Now discriminatory words are generally unacceptable and many people agree that social attitudes and equality has improved for women, ethnic minorities and LGBT people. Although there may still be a long way to go to achieve full equality, we have made progress.

The language used to describe intellectually disabled people has changed too, old terms such as 'idiot' or 'feeble-minded' originally were technical terms but later became insults, and so were replaced by newer, more scientific, terms such as 'mentally handicapped' (or 'mentally retarded' in the USA). Then, in the 1990s people argued that the term 'learning disabilities' improved understanding and it became widely used in the UK. Today, 'intellectual disabilities' is increasingly used to avoid confusion with people who have dyslexia or other learning difficulties. The important point to realise is that today's new and improved scientific term can become tomorrow's disrespectful insult. Unfortunately, whatever term is used seems to become viewed as offensive, because old attitudes persist.

Throughout history, some people with intellectual disabilities have behaved in ways other people found difficult, labelled as 'abnormal', 'aberrant', 'disordered', 'disturbed', 'dysfunctional' or 'maladaptive' behaviour. These older terms reflected the scientific understanding and social attitude to intellectually disabled people at the time, for instance maladaptive[1] means something bad that does not fit the environment. Dysfunctional means something that does not work or function. These words suggest a medical diagnosis of something wrong with person that was their fault. Therefore, the 'solution' was to try to fix the person, to punish them when they behaved badly, restrict them and lock them up in institutions. These terms reinforce bad attitudes that can result in bad treatment. Unfortunately, these attitudes are still around, even today. Whenever people are blamed for their behaviour that challenges they are at risk of abuse.

The abnormal, maladaptive, dysfunctional waiter

In a restaurant you try to attract the waiter's attention but they ignore you. Eventually, when they take your order, they are impatient, distracted, hardly speak to you, and don't smile. Then you have to wait a long time before they bring your food, which arrives cold with the wrong side order.

What would you think about the waiter?

Most people would probably think he was a rude, incompetent waiter. He did not do what a waiter should do, so he's 'dysfunctional'. As they got hungrier, they might have got angrier because it's the waiter's fault they had such bad service and think he should be punished rather than tipped.

However, would you think differently if you knew the following information?

The waiter worked until very late the night before, had very little sleep and has toothache. Just before you came in;

- the boss announced a waiters' pay cut and they have to handover tips
- four waiters should have been working but only two turned up
- 20 people arrived unexpectedly and ordered loads of food and drinks.

Most people would now think that there are good reasons for the waiter's behaviour, it's understandable and that probably he's usually quite pleasant and efficient but tonight is tired, stressed, overworked and in pain.

---

1 'Maladaptive behaviour' was used in the 1930s when eugenics was very influential, based on incorrect beliefs about race and evolution associated with the Nazis.

Key point: It's easy for any of us to blame someone for their behaviour when we don't know why they may be behaving in a particular way. We tend to go for simple solutions and ignore the complex situational factors, such as all the things going on in a person's environment and whether they are tired or in pain etc. We all blame others inappropriately sometimes, especially when we, ourselves, are stressed.

Why we use the term 'behaviour that challenges'

Originally, 'challenging behaviour' was a new term introduced in the 1990s based on improved scientific understanding of behaviour and the need to treat people more equally.

Behaviour means what we do, our actions, and is influenced by many different things. These things are of two main types:

1. **Things that are inside us or internal, such as our personal characteristics**, for example; our thoughts and emotions, physical and mental health, whether we are in pain, are anxious, tired or hungry, our past experiences, our skills and abilities, how we communicate, how much we understand, whether we have impairments or genetic conditions and so on.

2. **Things that are outside us or external, such as our physical and social environments**, for example; whether they are too hot, noisy, overcrowded, small, boring, how easily we get things we want or get away from things we don't like, who else shares our environment, how people treat and communicate with us, what things we have to do, how much help we get and so on.

Our actions are a result of how these internal and external factors affect one another. We are more likely to be friendly, happy and calm when we are not in pain or anxious, and in a comfortable environment with familiar people we like. We are more likely to get annoyed and aggressive when we are tired, hungry, in an unfamiliar restaurant served by a rude waiter, and wait ages for food. In both cases behaviour did not happen just because of internal things, but from a combination of internal AND external things.

We all learn by interacting with our environment, by doing something and seeing what happens. If a behaviour achieves something useful, we repeat it e.g. we learn that if we smile and say hello, people usually say hello back and give us attention. All behaviour serves a purpose, it is a way to communicate and control things. Even behaviour others find difficult functions to get us something or avoid something e.g. if someone is frightened when strangers stand too close, they may learn that hitting out usually makes them go away. If someone wants more attention, screaming loudly often makes people look. We all learn to adjust our behaviour depending on the environment to get our needs met. Behaviours that challenge can be the most efficient, e.g. if we hardly ever get attention, we learn that screaming rather than asking and being ignored can be the quickest and easiest way of getting it. So, the old terms 'dysfunctional' or 'maladaptive behaviour' are scientifically incorrect, because behaviours that challenges are functional adaptions to environments.

In the 1960s there was a growing realisation that everyone, even severely intellectually impaired people, can learn. This was very positive and eventually led to the term 'learning disability' being introduced. There were several campaigns for human rights and greater equality in the 1970s and 80s, and a recognition that people with learning disabilities and challenging behaviour were treated very unfairly, likely to be punished, over medicated, restrained and live hidden, in poor institutional environments. The new term 'challenging behaviour' emphasised a positive alternative view that the person's behaviour challenges us to provide better environments that enable them to get what they need without behaving in challenging ways, for example by ensuring people get more attention when they are behaving in appropriate ways to help them do something they enjoy. To do this, first we have to understand *why* behaviour happens, what things make the behaviour more likely and what it achieves for the person. This changed the aim from trying to 'fix' people, to improving environments in person-centred ways e.g. helping people move from large institutions to more typical 'ordinary' houses, using photos and signs to help people communicate, supporting people to do activities and learn skills to become more independent. Getting things right for a person usually means working on several of these environmental improvement strategies at the same time and also treating any health problems and addressing pain. This approach is much better than simply blaming the person, but is usually more complicated or challenging and has become known more recently as positive behavioural support (PBS).

However, debate about the best terms to use continues. Currently, some people criticise the use of 'challenging behaviour' as the term is often misunderstood and sometimes misused incorrectly as a diagnostic label. This is another example of how new, better terms can eventually become thought of as being offensive, because old attitudes continue despite changes in terminology. Recently the term 'behaviours that challenge' seems to be preferred to 'challenging behaviour'. These two terms are very similar and aim to convey the same helpful concepts and positive attitude. However, rather than simply changing a term it is also important that we understand and accurately explain their true meanings. We must also avoid using other inaccurate, disrespectful or harmful replacements, because we also have to continue to try and improve attitudes not just call things different names..

Defining behaviour that challenges

Definitions of behaviour that challenges

'Culturally abnormal behaviour of such an intensity, frequency or duration that the physical safety of the person or others is likely to be placed in serious jeopardy, or behaviour that is likely to seriously limit use of, or result in the person being denied access to ordinary community facilities.'
Emerson (1995, 2011)

'Behaviour of such an intensity, frequency or duration as to threaten the quality of life and/or the physical safety of the individual or others and is likely to lead to responses that are restrictive, aversive or result in exclusion.'
The Royal College of Psychiatrists (2007)

Key point: These definitions are very similar and complementary.

Both definitions are similar. They include the danger of harm to the person or other people and consider behaviours to be challenging because they make it more likely that the person will be punished, restrained or excluded. Both are 'social definitions' emphasising that it depends on what most other people in society think about the behaviour.

Behaviour that challenges is a social definition

Behaviour	Not challenging (socially acceptable)	Challenging (unacceptable)
Undressing	To go to bed	On public transport
Shouting and swearing	Watching a football match	In a church
Aggression	In a boxing ring	In a job interview
Temper tantrums	By a two-year-old child	By a 22 year old adult
Noncompliance	Refusing to give cigarettes to children	Refusing to let anyone be in the same room as you
Stereotypical meaningless repetitive body movements	In a disco	At airport security
Homosexuality	Today antidiscrimination laws protect gay people's rights e.g. same sex marriage is legal	Up until 1967 male homosexuality was illegal and continued to be considered a psychiatric disorder for some time

Key point: What is considered socially acceptable in one culture, community, place or time may be considered unacceptable in another, and these things can change.

What other things could make behaviour be considered challenging?

Both definitions also highlighted intensity, frequency or duration. Intensity is about what impact the behaviour has, for example, we may smash a plate in temper but to smash every window would be severe and challenging. Frequency means how often a behaviour occurs. Everyone occasionally loses their temper, for example, and can even be aggressive at times, but if this happens much more frequently, e.g. several times a day, then this is challenging. Duration means how long the behaviour lasts. Most people may behave in a particular way for short periods of time, e.g. shouting for a few minutes, but asking the same question repeatedly for hours on end, can be challenging.

How able the person is to explain why they behaved in a particular way is also important. If people can explain that they behaved badly because they were stressed for various reasons, then their behaviour is often considered reasonable, (remember the waiter). Many people with intellectual disabilities may have difficulties explaining why they may have done something, so other people are more likely to blame and punish them, rather than understand why.

The quality of the environment is one of the main reasons that people are viewed as having behaviour that challenges or not. Some key factors that affect this in services are summarised in Figure 1 below. A person who has a history of behaving in challenging ways is likely to behave very differently depending on whether they are supported by staff team A or B.

Staff team A have been helped to rise to the challenge of providing good quality PBS. A practice leader role models PBS working alongside staff, coaching them to support people to have a good quality of life and promoting teamwork. Staff understand each person well and provide active support to help people participate in activities at home and in the community. Staff have support from professionals and get help to cope with stress. Together they have created a homely person-centred environment where people don't need to use behaviours that challenge.

In contrast, **staff team B** provide poor quality support, have no clear approach or training and are expected to just get on with it. No one has helped them to understand the person or improve the environment. Staff don't help people to participate, people do very little, have a poor quality of life and use behaviour that challenges to get their needs met. Staff restrain them frequently and restrict what they do, e.g. they don't allow them into the kitchen, and only take them out when they've been 'good', so they hardly ever go out. Things get worse and everyone is stressed because there is a lot of behaviour that challenges. Staff don't want to work there and lots of unfamiliar temporary staff are used to cover shifts. The manager spends most time in an office doing paperwork and very little time with the team or people they support.

Figure 1: Whether a person is considered to have behaviour that challenges or not depends on how well they are supported

Staff team A ✔	A person with intellectual disabilities	Staff team B ✘
■ Practice leadership. ■ Induction and ongoing training. ■ Person-centred approach. ■ Positive behavioural support (PBS). ■ Active support – people spend most time engaged in activities they like. ■ Focus on quality of life. ■ Multidisciplinary support -behavioural specialist, speech and language, OT etc. ■ Stable confident staff team who know people well. ■ Frequent staff supervision. ■ Stress management. ■ Mindful staff.	■ Aggression ■ Self Injury ■ Non-compliance	■ Manager in office. ■ Very little relevant training. ■ No clear approach. ■ Restrictive practice. ■ Staff don't involve people. ■ Hotel model – people spend most time doing nothing or behaving in challenging ways. ■ Focus on physical restraint, and inappropriate medication. ■ No external support or scrutiny. ■ Unstable team – high levels of staff sickness and turnover. ■ Temporary staff who don't know people well. ■ Infrequent staff supervision. ■ Stressed, frightened staff.
High quality of life Less behaviour that challenges	Vs	Low quality of life High levels of behaviour that challenges

The key point is that environments make a difference. Staff team A think the people they support are quite able, although they may have a very occasional minor incident, they don't consider them to be challenging, and they like them. Staff team B may not like the people they support, they might think they are dangerous, and therefore should be frequently restrained for everyone's safety, be given stronger sedatives or moved to a secure hospital assessment and treatment unit.

Whenever you are trying to understand behaviour that challenges and how to help, try and put yourself in the person's shoes and think about what it would be like to experience things from their perspective.

> **Ask yourself a key question**
>
> If I was similar to them and living in the environment they live in, would I be likely to behave in a challenging ways?
>
> You may be surprised by how often your answer is YES!

Conclusion

The term 'behaviour that challenges' means not blaming the person for what they do, but thinking about these behaviours as a challenge for us to understand why they happen and how to improve the person's environment and well-being, so they no longer need to behave in challenging ways. This correct meaning of 'behaviour that challenges' is based on scientific evidence and ethical values, promoting a mind set that is the foundation of modern, person centred approaches such as positive behavioural support described in other chapters of this book.

Key learning points

- Behaviour that challenges is not a medical diagnosis.

- What makes a behaviour challenging is what people consider social acceptable, how severe, frequent, or how long it lasts.

- Behaviour that challenges can harm the person or those around them and make it more likely that the person is punished, restricted, restrained, over-medicated or excluded from society.

- All behaviour happens for a reason and functions as a way of communicating, getting or avoiding things that are important to the person.

- The challenge is for us to understand a person's behaviour and provide an environment where they have a good quality of life and can get their needs met in non-challenging ways.

References

Emerson E & Enfield SL (2011) *Challenging Behaviour*. Cambridge: Cambridge University Press.

NICE (2015) *Challenging Behaviour and Learning Disabilities: prevention and interventions for people with learning disabilities whose behaviour challenges NICE guideline* [online]. Available at: https://www.nice.org.uk/guidance/qs101/chapter/introduction (accessed February 2019).

Chapter 2: Behaviour that challenges: how big is the problem?

By Jonathan Mason

Summary

Differences in how behaviour that challenges is defined and measured, as well as the different circumstances people of different ages, cultures, living arrangements and diagnoses find themselves in, means that arriving at a single figure that describes 'the size of the problem' would be misleading. It seems that 10-20% of people with intellectual disabilities (ID) have behaviour that could be described as challenging, whereas the numbers are significantly higher in residential settings and in people in their teens and early 20s. There are many factors that contribute to the likelihood of a person engaging in behaviour that challenges, including individual factors (such as the person's health, mood and communication skills), and external or environmental factors (such as the quality of staff support, the suitability of the environment and the individual's overall quality of life).

When does behaviour become challenging?

In the previous chapter, Edwin Jones examines some of the different ways that behaviour that challenges can be described and defined. In this chapter, we'll focus on behaviour that meets Eric Emerson's (1995) well known definition of behaviour that challenges – behaviour that is a) culturally abnormal and puts the safety of either the person with intellectual disability or other people in serious jeopardy or b) behaviour that seriously limits the ability of the person with an intellectual disability to access ordinary community services.

A note on terminology

There are two terms that crop up in the literature about the frequency of behaviour that challenges that are helpful to understand – *prevalence* and *incidence*. *Prevalence* (sometimes referred to as point prevalence) is the number of 'cases' at any one time. In other words, if you take a cross section of any population (for example, children in school) and measure how many of them have a certain characteristic (such as behaviour that challenges), you arrive at a prevalence figure of some description (usually a percentage, sometimes a ratio, occasionally a number per 100,000). Generally, it's the prevalence rate expressed as a percentage that we are interested in when we are examining the size of a problem. If, however, you decide that you want to know how many children who start school at the beginning of the new school year have behaviour that challenges, you are seeking to understand the *incidence* rate.

Prevalence, then, is how many people overall demonstrate the characteristics you are interested in, whereas incidence is the number of *new* people that demonstrate the characteristics you are exploring– usually expressed as a percentage of the overall population being studied each year or two years. In this chapter, we'll focus on prevalence rates as the key metric for understanding the size of the problem.

Case study: a shift leader's dilemma

Jim, a shift leader with five years of experience running respite services for people with an intellectual disability, is coming to the end of four long days – 12 hours on shift, with just a couple of short breaks each day to grab a coffee and enjoy some down time, hoping that the phone does not ring. He is running a shift of three staff, supporting ten clients with moderate to severe intellectual disabilities in an accommodation service in the middle of a busy regional town. Like most days, there are some tough decisions to make…

Two of the younger clients are supposed to go out to the supermarket to help with the shopping, but an incident last week where one of them became distressed by the noise of the trolleys being moved in the carpark and damaged someone's car means that Jim may have to keep that client at home. But if that happens, the client will miss out, and probably become so annoyed that there will be a repeat of last Friday's verbal outburst that everyone is still recovering from, especially Sarah, the new girl on placement from the local university who was quite upset by the yelling. Better keep the windows shut, just in case.

And then there is everyone else to think about. It's unseasonably hot, so going outside means a great deal of preparation and, for some, discomfort. Not that it is much better in the house, but at least it is out of the sun. Perhaps, if he locks away the sharp knives and keeps the door shut so that one or two of the more unpredictable clients cannot wander in, a few of them could prepare some cold drinks and food in the kitchen.

Jim cannot decide what to do – it is going to be one of those days, he thinks. Sometimes, it feels like he is having to accept that something challenging is going to happen, and just choose which one is going to cause everyone the least disruption…

Reflection

Now that you've read the case study, reflect on these questions to help you start thinking about some of the factors that influence the way that the prevalence rate for behaviour that challenges in people with an intellectual disability is reported in the literature.

■ Jim is worrying about several different kinds of behaviour, most of which are concerning but not all of which would meet the definition of 'challenging'. It is important to make sure that the research that we base our prevalence rates on is measuring *behaviour that challenges*. Which do you think meet the definition used at the beginning of this chapter?

■ Some sub-groups of people, and certain care settings, are associated with higher prevalence rates of behaviour that challenges. Which age groups and which settings do you think are usually linked with higher prevalence rates?

■ Some other disorders that are commonly associated with intellectual disability are linked to an increased prevalence of behaviour that challenges – can you think of any?

Behaviour that challenges in human services – the overall picture

As you will have learned from your reading so far, the large variety of ways that research into the prevalence of behaviour that challenges in people with intellectual disabilities has been conducted, makes it difficult to arrive at a single figure. As you will have read, there are some sub-groups of people with an intellectual disability that appear to have a significantly higher prevalence rate of behaviour that challenges.

Let us start by looking at the overall numbers. One of the most effective ways of establishing the overall prevalence rate for behaviour that challenges is to use population-based data. In these studies, everyone with an intellectual disability who lives in the geographical area being studied are included, and from there the number with behaviour that challenges are determined. Whilst the few studies that take this approach (four of the most well-known are listed in the references at the end of this chapter, and summarised in Table 1) tend to use similar criteria for defining 'intellectual disability' (usually something like 'receiving some form of assistance for their disability needs'), it is still possible that the samples in each study are difficult to compare, even in terms of the level of intellectual disability that people included in the study have. More problematic, however, are the different ways that 'behaviour that challenges' is operationalised. For example, whereas the Emerson *et al* (2001) study, the Lundqvist study (2013) and the Bowring *et al* (2017) study summarised in Table 1 used different versions of a measure called the Behaviour Problems Inventory to identify the presence of different behaviour that challenges, the Jones *et al* study used a purpose-designed measure based on the definition of 'problem behaviour' from the DC-LD (a diagnostic measure devised by the Royal College of Psychiatrists), and also asked psychiatrists involved in the study to make a judgement about the existence of behaviour that challenges based on their clinical opinion. Clearly, the questions you ask will determine the answers that you get.

Table 1: The overall prevalence of behaviour that challenges in people with intellectual disabilities

Study	Who was included	Prevalence rates
Emerson *et al* (2001)	All people with an ID in two district health authorities in the UK.	10-15%
Jones *et al* (2008))	All adults with ID in Greater Glasgow, Scotland.	18 (DC-LD)-22 (opinion) %
Lundqvist (2013)	All adults with ID in Orebro county, Sweden.	18%
Bowring *et al* (2017)	All adults with ID in Jersey.	18%

In summary, the three most recent studies included above appear to tell us that, as far as all adults with an intellectual disability are concerned, approximately 1 in 5 are likely to exhibit behaviour that challenges. The lower figure reported by Emerson *et al* may reflect the inclusion of younger children and older adults in their sample, as both groups are less likely to engage in behaviour that challenges (see below). Jones *et al* also report a slightly higher figure (22%) for the prevalence of behaviour that challenges when based solely on the clinical judgement of the psychiatrists involved in their study, which is interesting and perhaps serves as a reminder of the need for a careful and standardised approach to assessment in this area (see the suggestions in Chapter 6). This is likely to be true for how the severity of someone's disability is assessed, as well the classification of their behaviour (read on to see how the severity of someone's intellectual disability can play an important role in altering the likelihood of them exhibiting behaviour that challenges).

Are there any groups with higher prevalence rates?

The literature on prevalence rates also includes some important findings on some of the other factors that appear to increase the prevalence of behaviour that challenges in people with an intellectual disability. These can also be thought of as additional risk factors and are summarised in Table 2.

As you may be able to see from Table 2, aside from the influence of age and gender the overall severity of someone's level of impairment appears to play an important role in predicting the likelihood of behaviour that challenges. Although factors such as communication skills, level of disability and an additional diagnosis of ASD have been identified as influencing prevalence rates independently of one another, it also seems reasonable to group these together in to a 'level of impairment' factor. You will also find some important observations on the role of communication in behaviour that challenges in Jill Bradshaw's chapter (see Chapter 7).

Table 2: risk factors that can increase the likelihood of behaviour that challenges

Risk factor	Finding
Age	Adolescents and young adults with an intellectual disability are more likely to engage in behaviour that challenges.
Autism spectrum disorder	People with an intellectual disability who have also been diagnosed with autism spectrum disorder are more likely to engage in behaviour that challenges.
Communication skills	People without verbal communication, and people with a limited understanding of verbal communication, are more likely to engage in behaviour that challenges.
Severity of intellectual disability	People with a severe or profound intellectual disability are more likely to engage in behaviour that challenges than those with a mild/moderate level of impairment.
Gender	Men are generally more likely to engage in behaviour that challenges.

The factors summarised in Table 2 all appear to be relatively robust research findings; most research studies that examine their influence agree that, to a greater or lesser extent, they appear to be particular factors that increase the prevalence rate of behaviour that challenges in people with an intellectual disability. There are some other factors that there is less agreement on that are also worth highlighting:

- *Living in residential care settings:* some studies have found that people with intellectual disabilities who live in residential accommodation services are more likely to engage in behaviour that challenges (NICE, 2015).

- *Co-occurring mental health problems:* ADHD, mood disorders and anxiety disorders have been found in some studies to be associated with higher rates of behaviour that challenges, as have sleep problems (NICE, 2015).

- *Co-occurring physical health problems:* the relationships between physical well-being and behaviour that challenges has been somewhat neglected in the literature. Pain, for reasons that most of us will be familiar with, has been identified by some studies to have a reasonably strong association with behaviour that challenges. Additionally, there is also evidence that those with behaviour that challenges are more likely to be using psychotropic medication, which can in turn lead to side effects (such as constipation) that have themselves been identified as risk factors for behaviour that challenges. Lastly, urinary incontinence appears as a risk factor for behaviour that challenges in a small number of studies (See De Knegt *et al* (2013) for an excellent review).

Are there any types of behaviour that challenges that are more common than others?

The population studies summarised in Table 1, and other studies that have looked at smaller or less representative groups (sometimes referred to as cohort studies) of people with intellectual disabilities and behaviour that challenges appear to identify a broad range of behaviours as being typical in clients who have behaviour that challenges, and no single behaviour reliably stands out as 'the most common'. However, differences between studies notwithstanding, generally speaking the most common types of behaviour that challenges are noted as being self-harming behaviours such as self-hitting and scratching, and verbal aggression. Physically aggressive or destructive behaviour and stereotyped behaviour (such as repetitive body movements and screaming) are also noted amongst the most common types of behaviour that challenges.

Severe behaviour that challenges

Some studies differentiate between behaviour that challenges and severe behaviour that challenges. Severe behaviour that challenges is defined in various ways in different studies, but usually includes people who have more than one behaviour in the 'severe' category. As one might expect, the prevalence rates for severe behaviour tend to be lower, and figures around 10% are commonly reported.

The influence of support staff attitudes, training and behaviour on prevalence rates

Perhaps unsurprisingly, the literature indicates that as well a range of individual and environmental factors that influence the prevalence of behaviour that challenges in people with intellectual disabilities, the approach to working with this population taken by support staff also plays an important role. Research by Hastings and Remington (1994) suggests that the attitude of support staff to people with intellectual disabilities in general, and to behaviour that challenges specifically, influences the way they interact with their clients, which can in turn help to increase or decrease the prevalence of the behaviour. When confronted with these behaviours, staff who hold domineering, harsh or resentful attitudes towards people with behaviour that challenges are less likely to interact with those clients, and as a result the behaviour can become harder to manage in both the short and long term.

What about behaviour that is problematic but not challenging?

As you read above, one of the measures that is used in some of the highest quality research studies examining prevalence rates is the Behaviour

Problems Inventory (Rojahn *et al*, 2001). Usually, when this measure is used, a behaviour is defined as 'challenging' if it is rated as 'severe' on the severity scale incorporated into the measure. As you might expect, once we start to consider a broader range of behaviours, or behaviours that occur at a lower level of severity, the prevalence rate goes up dramatically. Some studies have found that once behaviours that are less severe are included (in other words, behaviours are rated as having occurred, but necessarily at a 'severe' level of intensity), the reported prevalence rates increase to 50% and beyond.

Conclusion: so – how big is the problem?

There is a great deal of literature in this area, but only a handful of studies that take the 'total population' approach (the best way of understanding the true prevalence of behaviour that challenges in people with an intellectual disability). Interestingly, the findings between studies are relatively consistent, and we can expect approximately 20% of people with an intellectual disability to have at least one behaviour in the 'severe intensity' category, and to meet the definition of behaviour that challenges.

References

Bowring DL, Totsika V, Hastings RP, Toogood S & Griffith GM (2017) Challenging behaviour in adults with an intellectual disability: a total population study and exploration of risk indices. *British Journal of Clinical Psychology* **56** (1) 16–32.

De Knegt NC, Pieper MJC, Lobbezoo F, Schuengel C, Evenhuis HM, Passchier J and Scherder EJA (2013) Behavioural pain indicators in people with intellectual disabilities: a systematic review. *Journal of Pain* **14** 885–896.

Emerson E, Kiernan C, Alborz A, Reeves D, Mason H, Swarbrick R, Mason L & Hatton C (2001) The prevalence of challenging behaviours: a total population study. *Research in Developmental Disabilities* **22** (1) 77–93.

Hastings RP and Remington B (1994) Rules of engagement: toward an analysis of staff responses to challenging behavior. *Research in Developmental Disabilities* **15** (4) 279–98.

Jones S, Cooper A, Smiley E, Allan L, Williamson A & Morrison J (2008) Prevalence of, and factors associated with, problem behaviours in adults with intellectual disabilities. *The Journal of Nervous and Mental Disease* **196** (6) 678–686.

Lundqvist L (2013) Prevalence and risk markers of behaviour problems among adults with intellectual disabilities: a total population study in Orebro County, Sweden. *Research in Developmental Disabilities* **34** (4) 1346–1356.

National Institute of Health and Care Excellence (NICE) (2015) *Challenging Behaviour and Learning Disabilities: Prevention and interventions for people with learning disabilities whose behaviour challenges* [online]. Available at: https://www.nice.org.uk/guidance/ng11 (March 2019).

Rojahn J, Matson J, Lott D, Esbensen AJ & Smalls Y (2001) The behaviour problems inventory: an instrument for the assessment of self-injury, stereotyped behaviour, and aggression/destruction in individuals with developmental disabilities. *Journal of Autism and Developmental Disorders* **31** (6) 577–588.

Chapter 3: Positive behavioural support

By Anne McDonald

Summary

This chapter will provide a brief introduction to positive behavioural support (PBS) and will outline some ways of using PBS to support people with intellectual disabilities who present with 'behaviour that challenges'. PBS is a person-centred approach which provides a basis for understanding the message conveyed by behaviour that challenges. It is a framework which supports the development of strategies to support people with behaviour that challenges. PBS is based on the premise that behaviour can be changed, and that the most effective ways to change it are to adapt the environment to support the person better, and to teach the person different ways of behaving.

What is positive behavioural support?

PBS is a framework for supporting people with intellectual disabilities who have behaviour that challenges. It has been developed over the past 25 years and is regarded as best practice, recommended in a number of government policy documents and good practice guidance throughout the UK and beyond. It has been defined and described in a variety of studies over the years. The most common definition used in the UK was developed by Gore *et al* in 2013.

The components of positive behavioural support

Summarising the various definitions of PBS over the years leads us to four main components of a PBS approach:

1. **PBS is focused on improving quality of life**. This means that the most important goal of PBS is to improve the quality of life for individuals with behaviour that challenges; this includes improved relationships, greater opportunities, increased community integration, and a greater range of choices.

2. **PBS is based on a specific value base**. This means that there are a range of values which underpin PBS. These include:

   - that PBS is person-centred and uses interventions which are socially valued; a commitment to non-punishment-based approaches

   - that family, friends and direct care staff should be involved in the development of interventions

- that these interventions must fit with the values, resources and skills of those who will be carrying them out.

3. **PBS uses behavioural methods**. This means that there are a number of behavioural elements which must be included in a PBS approach. This includes the use of functional assessment and a PBS plan containing a range of different strategies (more details about both of these are outlined in this chapter).

4. **PBS is a system-wide approach**. This means that PBS is most effective and successful when it is implemented across a whole service or organisation, rather than just for an individual.

Using positive behavioural support

The process of using PBS with people with intellectual disabilities and behaviour that challenges generally begins with an assessment to understand the reasons for the behaviours occurring. This is called functional assessment, as it seeks to understand what *function* or *purpose* the behaviour serves for the person. Following on from the functional assessment, a PBS plan is then developed. This plan will contain a range of strategies to minimise the behaviour that challenges and improve the person's quality of life. More details about functional assessment and developing PBS plans are described below.

Step 1: functional assessment

Define the behaviour

The first stage of a functional assessment is to describe and define the behaviour clearly. Once the behaviour is clearly described and defined it, then we can begin to record when it happens, and through this process we can begin to understand why it happens. Behaviour that challenges should be defined clearly, so that different staff can all agree on what the behaviour is, and are all in agreement about when it has occurred.

Collect information

Once the behaviour is defined, there are a range of ways that information can be collected about the behaviour that challenges. The types of information recorded might include:

- Frequency (how often the behaviour happens).
- Duration (how long it lasts).
- Severity (how severe it is).

Information about behaviour that challenges is often collected via ABC forms. They describe the **A**ntecedents (what happens before the behaviour); the

Behaviour; and the Consequence (what happens after the behaviour). ABC forms can help identify the function of the behaviour.

Identify the function

Once information about behaviour that challenges has been collected, this can be used to identify the function or message of the behaviour for the person.

It is important to remember that a person can use the same behaviour to communicate a different message in different situations. For example, a person may hit out at staff, and in one situation, this could mean 'leave me alone', and in another situation, with different things happening in the environment around the person, this could mean 'come and talk to me'.

A person can also use several different behaviours to communicate the same message. For example, someone may scream and throw things, and at other times may hit herself; and both behaviours could be communicating the same message.

There are four functions of behaviour that challenges: attention, escape, sensory and tangible. These are described below with some information about the message that may be communicated by that function; situations where that function is more likely; and ideas for strategies that may help for each function.

Function	What's the message?	Situations where this may occur	Strategies that may help
Attention	Talk to me. I'm lonely. I'm bored. There's nothing happening. I want to have some fun.	■ If the person receives low levels of attention from staff. ■ If the person's day is dull or repetitive. ■ If the behaviour causes a big reaction from staff or others.	■ Teach the person to ask for attention in a different way. ■ Ensure the person has an interesting and active day. ■ Offer high levels of attention non-contingently.
Escape	I don't understand what's happening. I want to get out of here. Make this stop. Leave me alone. This is too difficult.	■ If the environment is chaotic and disorganised. ■ If the person finds it hard to understand verbal communication. ■ If there is lack of predictable routine in the person's life.	■ Teach the person to say they want to leave or for the activity to end. ■ Use clear communication that is suitable for the person. ■ Ensure that activities are structured and predictable.

Function	What's the message?	Situations where this may occur	Strategies that may help
Sensory	I like how this feels. This calms me down. I like how these lights look. This makes me feel good.	■ If the person is in an unstimulating environment. ■ If the person needs high or different types of sensory feedback. ■ If the person spends long periods of time on their own.	■ Provide a range of activities with stimulation that is suitable for the person. ■ Schedule time for sensory activity. ■ Use sensory activities as a way to build interaction.
Tangible	I want that object. I want that food. That item is important to me. I want what you have. I want to eat that.	■ If the person is in a rigid or controlling environment. ■ If restrictions are placed upon the person's diet or activity. ■ If the person has had limited opportunity to experience or to choose.	■ Give free access to preferred items. ■ Teach the person to get the item/food independently. ■ Teach the person how to ask for the item in a different way.

See Chapter 6 for more detail on assessment of behaviour that challenges.

Case study: Brian

Brian is a 19-year-old man an intellectual disability who lives with his mum, dad and sister. Brian left school at the end of last term and now receives six hours support on each weekday. He is supported on a two-to-one basis due to his behaviour that challenges. This support is based in the family home. The two staff come in to work each morning and spend time in the kitchen with a cup of tea, discussing how they want to spend the day with Brian. He does not participate in this discussion, and usually stays in the living room. Staff feel he could not tell them what he wants to do, so there is no point in asking him.

Mostly, Brian spends time going for walks with staff in the local park, or sometimes he uses a nearby café, across the road from his house. Brian currently has no involvement at any level in any domestic activities round the house and doesn't get involved in food preparation. The staff feel it would be too big a risk to have him in the kitchen, particularly since he is very motivated by food.

Staff report that it is difficult to find activities in which Brian engages. When he does engage in an activity such as playing a game, this will only last for a very short space of time and then he will walk away. Staff are unsure how to re-engage him and feel a bit anxious about persisting with the activity in case he becomes challenging. They feel it is best to leave him on his own at this point.

Brian has some verbal communication skills although these tend to be used repetitively and it is unclear how much he actually understands of the words he uses. In particular it is felt he does not understand concepts relating to time, →

e.g. 'in five minutes' or 'later'. Staff feel that Brian has difficulty in communicating, and frequently fails to respond when people speak to him. In school, staff used visual communication with Brian (Boardmaker symbols), but these have been lost since he left school.

Brian exhibits behaviour that challenges by banging the table and vocalising loudly and aggressively. He will hit himself in the face, slapping his cheek repetitively. If staff try to intervene, he will often begin to hit out at them too. These behaviours often happen if the living room is very noisy with the TV on, or when his family members come in and there are a lot of people in the room. It may also occur in the café, particularly when it is noisy or busy.

Staff respond to the behaviour by taking Brian out of the environment he is in, either returning home from the cafe, or taking him to his bedroom if he is at home. They often leave him there to calm down on his own.

Before you read on, stop and think about the following questions:

■ What message(s) do you think Brian is trying to communicate with his behaviour?

■ Which function(s) of behaviour fit best with the description of Brian's behaviour?

In this case study, it is likely that the function of Brian's behaviour is escape. This is due to the following factors:

■ Brian finds noisy and busy places difficult, so he often wants to get away from them.

■ Brian does not have a structured routine, so is never sure what is happening next; this may make him feel anxious.

■ Brian has limited verbal communication, and may not understand all of what staff say to him; it is likely this will add to his anxiety in some situations.

Step 2: positive behavioural support plans

Once the function of behaviour that challenges has been identified, then a PBS plan can be developed. This helps guide staff and carers as to how they should be supporting the person in relation to their behaviour that challenges.

There are a number of different formats available for PBS plans. However what they all have in common is that they contain both proactive and reactive strategies. A good PBS plan will have more proactive strategies than reactive strategies.

Proactive strategies

Proactive strategies are designed to improve the person's life, so that the person has access to the type of support that they need, and that over time, behaviour that challenges becomes unnecessary.

They should include:

Environmental changes: these are changes to the environment to make it more suitable for the person, and so that their needs can be met. This includes changes to the physical environment, as well as changes to the support the person receives, such as the activities they are offered, or the way that staff communicate with them. For these changes to be most effective, it is important that all staff work consistently with the person, particularly when new activities or communication methods are being introduced.

Teaching new skills: these are new skills or behaviours that the person can be taught so that they do not need to use behaviour that challenges. For this to be successful, the new behaviours need to be more effective for the person. For example, if a person challenges to get attention, and is taught to request attention by the use of a card with a symbol, then staff must ensure that they react to the use of the symbol card more promptly than they would for the behaviour that challenges.

Reactive strategies

These are to deal with the behaviour as it is occurring, to minimise risk and as far as possible to keep people safe. These may include:

De-escalation: these are techniques that might help a person calm down, e.g. giving the person some space, asking the person what's wrong, using a calm tone when talking to the person, using humour to calm a situation. These tend to be very person-specific, so it is a good idea to know what helps someone that you support to de-escalate.

Distraction: this is distracting the person from their behaviour that challenges, perhaps by offering an alternative activity, or by changing the stimulation in the room, or by changing the conversation.

Capitulation: this means giving the person what they want at that point, e.g. if the person wants to leave an environment, or to stop an activity that they find difficult, then you would just allow that to happen.

Before you read on, stop and think about what types of strategies you think might benefit Brian in the case study above.

1. What environmental changes could you make that would help Brian?

2. What kind of activities might you introduce to Brian?

3. How might you communicate differently with Brian?

4. What new skills would it benefit Brian to learn?

5. What kind of reactive strategies might be needed?

Remember:

■ PBS only uses strategies which are *socially valued*. This means something that other non-intellectually disabled people would enjoy doing and consider a valued activity.

■ PBS is committed to purely *positive approaches*. Any strategies which are aversive or use punishment should not be considered.

■ The main aim of PBS is to improve the person's *quality of life*.

Below is an outline of a PBS plan for Brian.

Proactive strategies		Reactive strategies
Environmental changes	New skills	
Create a structured week for Brian that has routine and is predictable, with a wider range of valued and enjoyable activities.	Teach Brian to use a Boardmaker symbol to say he wants an activity to stop, or wants to leave an environment.	Support Brian to leave the environment if it is too noisy.
Use Boardmaker symbols to help Brian understand what is happening throughout his day.	Teach Brian to use a visual timer, to help him understand how long activities will last.	Use his Boardmaker symbol to show you have understood he wants to leave.
Involve Brian in planning his day; use symbols to offer Brian choices about activities.	Teach Brian simple food preparation, e.g. how to make a sandwich.	Reassure Brian that you are going home, use a symbol to show this.
Find quieter times to take Brian to the café.		

Proactive strategies

Environmental changes

✔ **Structured week** – Brian's current support is unplanned and chaotic; it is likely he finds this difficult to cope with. Creating a more structured week with routine and predictability should help Brian feel less anxious.

✔ **Use of visual communication** – Brian had previously used Boardmaker symbols at school; reintroducing these would help him to understand what is happening throughout his day.

✔ **Providing choice** – giving Brian the opportunity to choose how he spends his day, and offering him preferred activities, may help him engage in activity for longer periods, and not use behaviour that challenges to end activities.

✔ **Quieter environments** – Brian finds noise and busy places difficult, so visiting the café at a quieter time will help him feel more comfortable there.

New skills

✔ **Sign for stop/leave** – Brian often challenges in order to make an activity stop or in order to leave an environment. Teaching him to communicate this in a different way may help him no longer need to use behaviour that challenges to communicate this message.

✔ **Visual timer** – Brian finds it difficult to know how long activities will last and this can cause him some anxiety. Teaching him to use a visual timer will give him a clear indication of how long any activity has still to go, and may help him feel less anxious.

✔ **Food preparation** – Brian is very motivated by food, so building food preparation into his daily routine is likely to be positive for him; this may be an opportunity for building positive relationships with staff, through sharing an enjoyable activity together.

Reactive strategies

✔ **Support to leave** – if Brian finds an environment too difficult it may be best to leave and try again another time, rather than trying to persuade him to stay and then a challenge occurring.

✔ **Sign for leaving** – encouraging Brian to use his Boardmaker sign for leaving may help him learn that this is a better way to communicate this, rather than using behaviour that challenges.

✔ **Home symbol** – at difficult times, visual communication can be more helpful in communicating a message than only verbal communication. It is likely that at this point Brian has become anxious and upset, so he may need you to use visual communication with him in order to reassure him.

See Chapters 9-15 for more information on types of intervention that may be used within a PBS plan.

Step 3: Evaluating positive behavioural support

An important part of PBS is its commitment to evaluating the impact of what we do. The final stage in using PBS is therefore to evaluate whether the strategies put in place have been successful. A good quality, well-implemented PBS plan should show changes both in the person's quality of life and in the person's behaviour that challenges.

These can be evaluated in different ways, including:

■ Using ABC forms to check whether the behaviour is happening less often than before the PBS plan was put in place. These could also be used to check if behavioural incidents are shorter, when they do occur.

- Comparing a week in the person's life before and after the PBS plan was introduced. This could tell us if the person is participating in more activities and if they have more valued activities.

- Talking to the person, or their family, or their staff, to ask them if things feel better than before. The person may be able to say if they feel happier and if their support is working better for them. Carers are also often a good source of evaluation, as they will know whether the situation feels improved and if they are experiencing less behaviour that challenges.

Key learning points

- The main goal of PBS is to improve quality of life for the person with intellectual disabilities and behaviour that challenges. A secondary goal is to decrease incidents of behaviour that challenges.

- The starting point of PBS is to understand what the behaviour that challenges means for the person, and what message the behaviour communicates. This is usually done by carrying out a functional assessment.

- Functional assessment tells us the function or reason for the behaviour. There are four functions of behaviour:

  - To gain **attention** or interaction from others.
  - To **escape** from a situation or task or environment.
  - To experience **sensory** stimulation.
  - To gain a **tangible** item.

- Following on from understanding the function of the behaviour that challenges, PBS then suggests a range of proactive and reactive strategies which will help to minimise the behaviour that challenges and improve the person's quality of life.

- These new strategies must be introduced systematically and consistently. They are most likely to be successfully if used by everyone who supports the person.

- It is important to evaluate the impact of the new strategies, to see whether these are achieving positive outcomes for the individual. The main positive outcomes sought are that the person has a better quality of life (e.g. more enjoyable activities, more positive experiences, better relationships with those around them, a better way of communicating) and also that their behavioural challenges are occurring less often.

Reference

Gore N, McGill P, Toogood S, Allen D, Hughes JC, Baker P, Hastings R, Noone SJ, Denne LD (2013) Definition and scope for positive behavioural support. *International Journal of Positive Behavioural Support* **3** (2) 14-23.

Further reading

Allen D, James W, Evans J, Hawkins S & Jenkins R (2005). Positive behavioural support: definition, current status and future directions. *Learning Disability Review* **10** 4-10.

Carr EG, Dunlap G, Horner RH, Koegel RL, Turnbull AP, Sailor W, Anderson JL, Albin RW, Koegel LK & Fox L (2002) Positive behavior support: evolution of an applied science. *Journal of Positive Behavior Interventions* **4** (1) 4-16.

La Vigna GW & Willis TJ (2005) A positive behavioral support model for breaking the barriers to social and community inclusion. *Learning Disability Review* **10** (2) 16-23.

PBS Academy. Resources for family carers, people with learning disabilities, support workers, service providers, & commissioners. Available at: http://pbsacademy.org.uk/ (accessed March 2019).

Chapter 4: Legal considerations

By Rachel Forrester-Jones

People tend to get a little nervous when we talk about the 'law'. This chapter is intended to help you understand the law in relation to supporting vulnerable adults (those aged 18 and over) with learning disabilities who have behaviour that challenges. A series of questions which you might ask yourself are hopefully answered below.

Is there a special law for people with 'behaviour that challenges'?

There is no specific law for behaviour that challenges. However, a set of laws (Acts of Parliament) exists which regulates other people's actions and inactions towards 'vulnerable adults' including those with behaviour that challenges. These laws protect people with behaviour that challenges and those who support them, including people working for local authorities and NHS services. Underpinning UK laws are the legal 'rights' set out in the European Convention of Human Rights (ECHR), in the form of various 'articles', all of which were incorporated into the Human Rights Act (HRA) (1998). Some of the articles are listed in the following pages. Remember, these legal rights are relevant to everyone, *including* people with learning disabilities who have behaviour that challenges.

Article 2 – the right to life

If a person's right to life is violated the state has a legal obligation to investigate. This includes when people die due to deficient and unsafe care. In the case of Connor Sparrowhawk who died in an NHS care unit, Southern Health trust were found to be guilty of breaching health and safety laws (Verita, 2015).

Article 3 – the right not to be tortured or suffer inhuman or degrading treatment

This relates to 'safeguarding', meaning that people with behaviour that challenges are protected in law from physical or mental abuse or neglect, from living in unacceptable and unsafe conditions, and from being humiliated by others such as those who are paid to care for them. Staff who abused people with learning disabilities, complex needs and behaviour that challenges at Winterbourne View care home were found to be criminally liable under UK law (Hill, 2012).

Article 5 – the right to liberty and security of person

This means that no one should be deprived of their liberty unless it is in accordance with the law (see the section in this chapter on whether people with behaviour that challenges can have their freedom legally restricted).

Article 6 – the right to a fair trial

It may be necessary for a person with a learning disability and behaviour that challenges to give evidence in court; so that they can tell the court what they witnessed to enable a fair hearing of the case, and where their welfare would not be prejudiced by doing so (Courts and Tribunals Judiciary, 2008). In addition to the ECHR, the UN Convention on the Rights of Persons with Disabilities (Article 13: access to justice), the Disability Discrimination Act (1995) the Equality Act (2010), and case law (see *R* v *Baker* [2010] EWCA Crim 4, [2010] ALL ER (D) 136 (Jan)) all require courts to make 'reasonable adjustments' for 'vulnerable adults' so that they can access and participate in court and give evidence in the best way that they can (see *R* v *James Michael Watts* [2010] EWCA Crim 1824 and the *Equal Treatment Bench Book* (Judiciary College, 2018)). Part II of the Youth Justice and Criminal Evidence Act (1999) specifies a range of 'special measures' for 'vulnerable witnesses'. These are: screens to obscure the defendant from the witness; giving evidence via live television links from outside the court; clearing the public gallery and excluding the press so that evidence can be given in private; removal of the judge's and barristers' wigs and gowns in Crown Court; video recorded police interviews used as evidence in chief; the option for cross examination to be recorded in advance of the trial; support from 'intermediaries' (e.g. speech and language therapists); and communication aids. Courts and tribunals also have safeguarding responsibilities and the judge is under a duty to intervene where necessary (including constraining the length, tone and wording of cross-examination; (*R* v *Lubemba, R* v *JP* (2014, EWCA Crim2064)) and to ensure the complainants vulnerability is not take advantage of (*R* v *Stephen Hamilton* [2014] EWCA Crim 155 [2014]).

The Coroners and Justice Act (2009) (following the Bradley Report (Department of Health, 2009)) also specifies that vulnerable adult defendants should have access to registered intermediaries to help them prepare for court as well as during proceedings. Failure to make reasonable adjustments could lead to a case being overturned on appeal.

Article 8 – the right to respect for a private and family life

This means that regardless of behaviour that challenges, people still have the right to make an informed choice about whether or not to have friendships, loving and sexual relationships, and to marry and have children, provided they have the capacity to consent and are not being abused.

Article 14 – the right to not be discriminated against in relation to all the other human rights set out in the ECHR

People with behaviour that challenges should not be treated differently (direct discrimination) in relation to any of their rights; including indirect discrimination (when a rule or policy disadvantages a particular group of people).

All these rights form the guiding principles of government policies and programmes specific to learning disabilities, such as: *Valuing People* (Department of Health, 2001); *Valuing People Now* (Department of Health, 2009); *The Government's Mandate to NHS England for 2018-19* (Department of Health and Social Care, 2018*); Transforming Care: A national response to Winterbourne View Hospital* (Department of Health, 2012) and *Building the Right Support* (2015); and *Improving Lives* (Department for Work and Pensions/ Department of Health, 2017) (see PQ 1333523, 28 March 2018). These policies and programmes all promote individual choice and equal access to services. Similarly, 'best practice' models of support such as positive behaviour support and person-centred planning have these fundamental rights at their core.

A range of standards and responsibilities that public agencies and people working in social services are expected to follow also exist. For example, under the Care Act (2014), local authorities (LAs) (i.e. a county council or district council in England, a London borough, or the Common Council of the City of London) have a general duty to promote an individual's well-being.

Does a person with behaviour that challenges also have a legal right to an assessment of their needs?

Yes. Under the Care Act (2014) each LA has a legal duty to assess a person with behaviour that challenges if they appear to be struggling with normal daily activities (e.g. dressing, cooking) without community care support. The LA can provide support before the assessment has taken place if the need for it is urgent.

To be lawful, the assessment has to consider how to improve or maintain the person's 'well-being' including their: dignity; mental and emotional health; protection from abuse and neglect; control and choice over their day-to-day life; ability to participate in education, work, training or recreation; social and economic well-being; social and family relationships; the suitability of their living accommodation; and their contribution to society.

The assessment must be completed within a 'reasonable time frame' (around four to six weeks from when the request was made), and carried out by a competent and trained assessor (e.g. a social worker). It should also be person centred; starting with the assumption that the person themselves knows best about their own needs, and involving them (with appropriate support from an independent advocate if necessary) in every aspect of their assessment. The Care Act (2014) stipulates that if an individual has 'substantial difficulty' in participating in their own assessment and care-plan, an 'appropriate individual' (e.g. a relative) or independent advocate should be asked about the person's needs (including communication requirements). The assessment should involve all relevant carers including family members.

The input of an expert (e.g. psychologist, psychiatrist, specialist behaviour nurse) may be required to ensure that the person's needs are fully understood and noted within the assessment (Department of Health and Social Care (2018a)). The expert may also conduct a 'functional assessment' of the person's behaviour. They will describe and analyse the type of behaviour that challenges (e.g. frequently hitting others or hitting themselves; destroying objects) and assess what might be triggering it, including the impact of the environment (e.g. building, light, noise, other people), any past trauma, or anything else that might help explain the behaviour. They will also describe and analyse the purpose the behaviour that challenges serves the person (e.g. to communicate a message, or gain the attention of someone else). See Chapter 3: Positive behavioural support for more details.

The LA has a duty to meet all of the person's 'eligible needs' identified in the assessment. 'Eligible needs' refer to those tasks a person is 'unable' to do on their own if unsupported. The Care Act defines 'unable' to achieve a daily living outcome as follows:

- Unable to achieve it without assistance.

- Able to achieve it without assistance but doing so causes the adult significant pain, distress or anxiety.

- Is able to achieve it without assistance but doing so endangers or is likely to endanger the health and safety of the adults, or of others; or

- Is able to achieve it without assistance but takes significantly longer than would normally be expected.

(The Care and Support (Eligibility Criteria) Regulations 2015 no. 313 para 2 s(2))

To be eligible for support, the person has to have two or more of the following 'eligible needs':

- Managing and maintaining nutrition.

- Maintaining personal hygiene.

- Managing toilet needs.

- Being appropriately clothed.

- Being able to make use of the adult's home safely.

- Maintaining a habitable home environment.

- Developing and maintaining family or other personal relationships.

- Accessing and engaging in work, training, education or volunteering.

- Making use of necessary facilities or services in the local community including public transport, and recreational facilities or services.

- Carrying out any caring responsibilities the adult has for a child.

The LA must meet the person's identified needs by using a person-centred and person-led 'care and support plan' (a document stating how the LA will meet the person's needs, what support will be provided, how often, and by whom) and/or a 'positive behavioural support plan' (step-by-step instructions to help reduce behaviour that challenges and improve the person's quality of life). The individual and their family/carers should agree the plan and it should be reviewed at least annually. If the individual or their family do not think the support plan will improve their well-being, they can complain to the LA. If that does not resolve the issue then a complaint can be made to the local government ombudsman. Alternatively, legal advice can be sought. A family can apply for judicial review of decisions around care and support though these need to be issued promptly (within three months of the date the decision was made by the LA).

Who pays for the support?

The LA will carry out a financial 'eligibility' assessment to determine whether or not the person with behaviour that challenges needs financial assistance to pay for their care. If they cannot afford to pay, the LA will meet the cost. Even if the individual is not financially eligible, the LA should still arrange the care. Where the LA are paying, the care and support/behaviour plan will include details of a 'personal budget' (the amount of money the LA will have to pay for the services needed as set out in the care and support plan). The personal budget can be used in the following ways:

- The LA may directly provide a particular service e.g. a LA or charity day centre placement each week; or

- Cash payments (called 'direct payments') will be given to the adult (or their family if they lack capacity to budget themselves) to employ services and carers directly. A local direct payment support service (DPSS) is also normally available to help families manage these payments. This is called a 'managed account'; Or

- A third party/broker (this could be a service provider) will manage the personal budget. Similar to a managed account, this is usually called an 'individual service fund'.

If the individual with behaviour that challenges has additional health and housing needs, the LA must notify the NHS or housing authority who will carry out their own assessments. The LA, NHS and other relevant agencies have a legal duty under the NHS Act (2006) and the Care Act (2014) to co-operate with one another to ensure that the person's needs are met.

For people with 'a primary health need', e.g. complex psychological or behavioural difficulties that require specialist care, or complex medication or feeding needs etc, they may be eligible for NHS 'continuing healthcare'. Unlike social care, this type of medical care will be free regardless of the person's financial circumstances and it can also be paid as a personal health budget (the individual agrees with the NHS how the money will be spent) or as a direct payment. A nurse assessor using a 'decision support tool' will assess on a continuum from 'no needs' to 'priority needs' a number of medical need 'domains' including the following:

- Breathing.
- Nutrition: food and drink.
- Continence.
- Skin and tissue viability.
- Mobility.
- Communication.
- Psychological and emotional needs.
- Cognition.
- Behaviour.
- Drug therapies, etc.
- Altered states of consciousness.
- Other significant care needs.

(Department of Health and Social Care (2018) p6 para 20, Fig1)

If the person does not get NHS continuing healthcare, the NHS and the LA may agree to 'joint funding' the care. If the LA or NHS do not meet the individual's needs according to the support plan (including providing a cheaper service which is less beneficial to the person's well-being) they are acting unlawfully and families can make a formal or legal complaint.

What about when a person's behaviour is criminal?

If someone has capacity to make a decision about their behaviour then, under the Mental Capacity Act (2005), they are regarded as responsible for their actions, including criminal acts. If a person with behaviour that challenges has been arrested for a crime, the Police and Criminal Evidence Act (PACE) (1984) specifies that a person should be treated as 'mentally vulnerable' if they are unable to understand: the significance of what is said to them (by the police officer); questions put to them; or their own replies. In this case, a responsible person (called an 'appropriate adult' (AA)) should be called to support them. AAs must not work for the police and in some areas there are independent AA services. Alternatively, paid carers, family members, social workers, trained volunteers and members of the public can fulfil this role, which is to ensure the person who has been arrested understands that the AAs role is to support and protect them and understands what is happening to them. AAs will support them during police questioning and help them with communication. The AA should also note whether the police are acting fairly as regards the individual's legal rights and ensure that the individual knows and understands their legal rights (Home Office, 2003).

Where concerns about a defendant's mental capacity are raised, a 'fitness to plead' hearing can be held in the crown court (Domestic Violence, Crime and Victims Act (2004)). The criteria used to determine fitness to plead (from *R* v *Pritchard* (1836) 7 C&P 303) are:

- capacity to plead with understanding
- ability to follow the proceedings
- knowing that the juror can be challenged
- ability to question the evidence
- ability to instruct counsel (barristers).

Legally, the person need only lack capacity for one of the criteria above to be regarded as unfit to plead. Yet *with* support individuals may be fit to plead and able to engage fully in court proceedings. If, even with support, they are still unfit to plead, then a 'trial of the facts' is held, at which the jury decides whether or not the defendant is guilty of the act or omission (failing to act in a particular way). Under the Domestic Violence, Crime and Victims Act (2004) s24, the court will choose one of the following outcomes (called 'disposals'):

- An order for absolute discharge.
- A supervision order.
- A hospital order under the Mental Health Act (1983) (amended 2007).

If the behaviour that challenges is of a sexual nature (e.g. sexual abuse of another person/s) then The Sexual Offences Act (2003) is the relevant law.

Can people with behaviour that challenges have their freedom legally restricted?

There are various ways in which a person with behaviour that challenges might have their freedom legally restricted, both in hospital and in the community, but there are legal processes and conditions which must be adhered to for any restrictions to be legal.

If the person with behaviour that challenges has the capacity to decide whether to be admitted to hospital, they cannot be forced to go unless they are suffering from a mental disorder (e.g. bipolar disorder or schizophrenia) and/or their behaviour is so 'abnormally aggressive or seriously irresponsible' that it poses a risk to their own or other's health and safety. In this case, a Mental Health Act (MHA) (1983) (revised 2007) assessment will be carried in hospital or in the community by two doctors (one must be an approved psychiatrist), and a LA approved mental health professional (AMHP) who is specifically trained in the MHA. Under section 2 of the MHA, the person with behaviour that challenges can be detained in hospital for up to 28 days for assessment and for up to six months for treatment (s3 MHA). Alternatively, the person may be supervised by the local social services authority in the community (a 'community treatment order') but they will return to hospital if they do not comply with the order. Just like anyone else, the person with behaviour that challenges has the right to appeal, the right to legal representation, and the right to an independent mental health advocate to challenge being detained in this way.

People who do not fall under the MHA may still be admitted to hospital under the Mental Capacity Act (MCA) (2005). For this to happen, firstly, a mental capacity assessment has to be carried out to determine whether they have capacity to decide to be admitted to hospital. If they have capacity they can choose to refuse to go to hospital. If they lack capacity to make this decision, another assessment will be made to make sure that hospital admittance is in their 'best interest'.

A residential care home or a hospital may wish to restrict the freedom of a person 'in their best interests' if they lack the capacity to understand their actions. An example of such a situation would be if the person has a tendency to run out of the care home into a busy road. To prevent an accident, the care home might wish to utilise door locks/key pads, which might effectively deprive the person of their liberty (e.g. if this meant that the person hardly ever went out of the home into the community). Any limitations on their freedom must be proportionate to the risk of harm to themselves, and necessary in order to carry out their care and support plan in their best interests. In order for a planned restriction to an individual's liberty to be lawful, it must be authorised by the LA and the Deprivation of Liberty application must be compliant with the Deprivation of Liberty Safeguards (DoLS) (2009) (an amendment to the Mental Capacity Act (2005)) (schedule A1)). Once the LA has received the application, assessors (approved MHA doctors and health professionals, and trained 'best interest assessors') will look at the proposed DoL to make sure the following conditions are met under the safeguards:

■ The person is 18 or over (different safeguards apply for children).

■ The person is suffering from a mental disorder.

■ The person lacks capacity to decide for themselves about the restrictions which are proposed so they can receive the necessary care and treatment.

■ The restrictions would deprive the person of their liberty.

■ The proposed restrictions would be in the person's best interests.

■ Whether the person should instead be considered for detention under the Mental Health Act.

■ There is no valid advance decision to refuse treatment or support that would be overridden by any DoLS process. (See *Mental Capacity Act (2005): Deprivation of Liberty Safeguards – Code of Practice* to supplement the main Mental Capacity Act (2005) Code of Practice, issued by the Lord Chancellor on 26 August 2008 in accordance with sections 42 and 43 of the Act (Ministry of Justice, 2008)).

If any of the above conditions are not met, DoL will not be authorised and the care home or hospital will need to change the person's care plan so that they can be supported in a less restrictive way. In this way, DoLS 'may also serve the purpose of protecting people who have capacity from being inappropriately detained or deprived' (Blamires *et al*, 2017: 715).

If all conditions are met, the DoL will be authorised and a person with behaviour that challenges may be deprived of their liberty for up to 12 months with 'conditions' (e.g. regular staff support to access community activities and/ or allowing relatives to visit the person in their home). The hospital or care home must explain the DoL authorisation (using appropriate alternative communication aids such as signs and symbols or photographs and pictures) to the person with behaviour that challenges, as well as their right to challenge the order through the Court of Protection. A legal representative (paid or unpaid person who knows the individual well) will be appointed to represent them, maintain contact and support; making sure that any conditions are carried out. The DoL order may be reviewed at any time and the hospital or care home can end the order at any time.

Following the leading case of *P* v *Cheshire West and another (Respondent)* [2014] UKSC 19 the Supreme Court provided the following test to decide if someone without capacity had been deprived of their liberty unlawfully:

1. They are subject to continuous supervision and control; and

2. They are not free to leave (with the focus being not on whether a person seems to be *wanting* to leave, but on how those who support them would react if they did want to leave).

Examples of where staff may detect unlawful deprivation (without safeguards and unauthorised) includes (paraphrased here for ease of understanding):

■ Where the LA forces a person with behaviour that challenges into a care home without their consent or against their will.

■ Where staff supervise and control the person's care and movements on an almost constant basis or for significant periods of time.

■ Where staff control the person's assessments, treatment, social contacts and residence (i.e. the care is overly restrictive or risk averse).

■ Where the person or their family/friends are not allowed to be involved in the DoL authorisation process.

■ Where the person or their family/friends are not happy with their loved one's care.

■ Where staff place such restrictions on the person that they cannot maintain contact with their family.

■ Where the person loses their independence.

■ Where the person is restricted from gaining access to the community.

■ Where the person or their family/friends are not told how to complain about their care (see DoLS Code of Practice (Ministry of Justice, 2008)).

In the judgement given on the case of *P* v *Cheshire West and Chester Council* P19 para 46, Lady Hale summed up the issue around deprivation of liberty:

'But, as it seems to me, what it means to be deprived of liberty must be the same for everyone, whether or not they have physical or mental disabilities. If it would be a deprivation of my liberty to be obliged to live in a particular place, subject to constant monitoring and control, only allowed out with close supervision, and unable to move away without permission even if such an opportunity became available, then it must also be a deprivation of the liberty of a disabled person. The fact that my living arrangements are comfortable, and indeed make my life as enjoyable as it could possibly be, should make no difference. A gilded cage is still a cage.'

Currently DoLS may only be used in relation to care homes or hospitals. In other settings, the applications for DoL must be made to the Court of Protection.

What about every day decisions?

Under the Mental Capacity Act everyone is assumed to have capacity unless it is proved that they do not have capacity. The MCA helps to assess this. The assessor is usually the person who is working with the person in relation to making a particular decision (including major decisions such as who to live with, as well as every day decisions, such as what to eat for breakfast). This will most often be a member of staff and they will need to consider that:

1. The person should have all the information they need to make a decision (e.g. they would need to see what choices of cereal they have in order to choose one, and any alternative breakfast food).

2. Some people with behaviour that challenges may need extra support to make a particular decision (e.g. who to live with in the supported living house).

3. Some people may need the information to be communicated in a way which they understand (e.g. using photographs, pictures or signs and symbols, and extra time to understand the information).

4. That the individual can understand and remember the information provided to them, and weigh up the advantages and disadvantages of any decision. The assessor can check this by asking various questions of the individual.

5. The individual may need additional support by e.g. another care worker, to help them in this assessment process.

If the person with behaviour that challenges has capacity, then they can make the decision themselves. If they have been assessed as lacking in capacity for a particular decision, then the decision can be made for them by a member of staff 'in their best interests', although the individual's past and present wishes, beliefs and values should be considered, and the least restrictive option possible should be chosen. For some decisions (such as who the person will share a house with, or medical interventions), a best interest meeting including all those who are involved with the person's care, including social workers and nurse professionals, should be convened to decide on whether or not the decision is in the person's best interests. Family members of the person with behaviour that challenges must, by law, be involved in these 'best interest' decisions (Mental Capacity Act (2005)).

In England and Wales very personal decisions (such as sexual relationships, marriage, adoption and voting) cannot be made using 'best interests'; only the person with capacity can make them. Some decisions can only be made by the Court of Protection (e.g. non-therapeutic sterilisation).

Conclusion

The law is 'live' – new legislation is enacted and amended, and case law sets new precedents For example, as this book goes to press, a Mental Capacity (Amendments) Bill [HL] 2017-19 is awaiting Royal Assent to reform DoLS. The information in this chapter is therefore likely to change. However, it has hopefully provided information to help staff working with people with behaviour that challenges understand laws which support and protect the legal status of such people, including those who lack capacity to make decisions about their lives and how they behave.

References

Blamires K, Forrester-Jones R and Murphy G (2017) An investigation into the use of the deprivation of liberty safeguards with people with intellectual disabilities. *Journal of Applied Research in Intellectual Disabilities* **30** (4) 414–726.

Court and Tribunals Judiciary (2008) *The Child, Vulnerable Adult and Sensitive Witnesses Practice Direction* [online. Available at: https://www.judiciary.uk/publications/pd-child-vulnerable-adult-sens-witnesses/ (accessed March 2019).

Department of Health (2001) *Valuing People – A New Strategy for Learning Disability for the 21st Century*. London: DH publishing.

Department of Health (2009) *Valuing People Now: A new three-year strategy for learning disabilities*. London: DH publishing.

Department of Health (2012) *Transforming Care: A national response to Winterbourne View Hospital*. London: DH publishing.

Department of Health & Social Care (2018a) *Care and Support Statutory Guidance*. London: DH & SC.

Department of Health & Social Care (2018b) *The Government's Mandate to NHS England for 2018 to 2019*. London: Department of Health and Social Care.

Department for Work and Pensions & Department of Health (2017) *Improving Lives: The future of work, health and disability Cm 9526*. London: HMSO.

Government & NHS England (2015) *Building the Right Support*. London: NHS England.

Hill (2012) Winterbourne View care home staff jailed for abusing residents [online]. *The Guardian* **26 October**. Available at: https://www.theguardian.com/society/2012/oct/26/winterbourne-view-care-staff-jailed (accessed March 2019).

Home Office (2003) *Guidance for Appropriate Adults*. London: HO.

Judicial College (2018) *Equal Treatment Bench Book*. Judicial College.

Ministry of Justice (2008) *Mental Capacity Act 2005: Deprivation of liberty safeguards - Code of Practice to supplement the main Mental Capacity Act 2005 Code of Practice*. Available at: https://webarchive.nationalarchives.gov.uk/20110322122009/http://www.dh.gov.uk/en/Publicationsandstatistics/Publications/PublicationsPolicyAndGuidance/DH_085476 (accessed March 2019).

Verita (2015) *Independent Review into Issues that May Have Contributed to the Preventable Death of Connor Sparrowhawk*. Available at: https://www.england.nhs.uk/wp-content/uploads/2015/10/indpndnt-rev-connor-sparrowhawk.pdf (accessed March 2019).

Further reading

Lord Bradley (2009) *The Bradley Report*. London: Department of Health Publications.

United Nations (2008) *Convention on the Rights of Persons with Disabilities*. Available at: https://www.un.org/development/desa/disabilities/convention-on-the-rights-of-persons-with-disabilities.html (accessed March 2019).

Chapter 5: Listening to people using services

By Tony Osgood

Summary

Behaviour carries meaning, no matter how disruptive or dangerous, and it might be considered as complaining, telling us something isn't working for the person. This chapter suggests that listening to the voices and stories of people using services, interpreting their behaviours as communication, is helpful for crafting good support.

Behaviour that challenges as a symptom

Behaviour that challenges may be thought of as communicating messages concerning the quality of life and the health and happiness of the person. Think of such behaviour as 'exotic communication': whilst unconventional it is effective, because people respond to seeing or being someone harmed (Ephraim, 1998). We can ignore a request, seldom a bite.

> **Case study: Amal**
>
> Family members and personal assistants have supported Amal at home for many years. Following an increase in behaviour that challenges, the twenty five year old arrives at a new service. Amal has limited verbal communication but is clearly distressed. The service is far from home and the people she knows and far from ideal, but it is the only service willing to offer Amal temporary respite. Amal arrives with her clothes, support plans written by personal assistants and family, and copies of assessments completed by her social worker.
>
> The service team work hard to make sense of the information, but the manager feels the documents are vague and contradictory: she gets no sense of Amal as a person. Two workers are allocated to create support strategies based on what they learn from spending time with Amal: what works, and what doesn't, in making Amal happy. The most urgent need is to understand Amal's screaming and hand biting. The team try different approaches and new activities in order to gauge Amal's responses.

Behaviour that challenges is a symptom of an unquiet and unhappy life. Behaviour that challenges keeps happening because it gains or avoids things better than anything else the person currently knows. This does not imply the person intends to convey anything, but any behaviour becomes meaningful if we think it is telling us something and respond accordingly. Often behaviour that challenges is viewed as a problem to solve not a message to be understood (Pitonyak, 2005). Behaviour that challenges is telling us the person has few other ways in which to exert choice and control.

Person-centred support

To understand behaviour that challenges fully is to appreciate not merely antecedents and consequences but the *contexts* that influence a person. Contexts include the preferences of people, their history, their goals, their ability to make choices that are respected, and their communication and social preferences. These contexts describe their story: who they are and where they come from. To be person-centred is to understand conflicts between the person's story and the support they receive, and to work in a manner that reduce such contradictions.

Some people communicate in ways that are difficult to interpret. We are then required to invest time and imagination to try out things we suspect the person will welcome. Such things must enhance the dignity of the person and improve their quality of life. The person's responses to our best efforts will tell us whether we're on the right course or need to change tack. Slowly, we develop an understanding of what the person prefers. By paying careful attention to their reactions we can create support strategies. We soon develop a significant list of things that the person responds well to, including:

- places and spaces the person enjoys

- people, communications and the type of interactions the person welcomes

- favourite activities, items and routines to which the person responds positively.

The team employ ABC records (antecedents, behaviours and consequences) to understand behaviour that challenges: when and where it occurs, what is happening at the time, what predicts it and what follows. This helps them evidence what they believe Amal's behaviour is communicating. After two weeks they find regular patterns. They learn:

1. Following a disturbed night, when woken for the morning routine by staff who are quite directive, Amal is likely to scream; Amal stops screaming once people leave her in peace. Amal doesn't scream if she has slept well, if staff are less directive, have more time to gently wake Amal with a drink, and sing with her.

2. Amal bites her hand when she has had no support for fifteen minutes or sees others talking or enjoying activities. Before hand-biting, Amal may scream. Hand-biting usually only happens after lunch and before dinner. Hand-biting gains attention, and often, activities.

Screaming in the morning means, 'I'm tired and don't like how I'm being supported'. Screaming in the afternoon means, 'I'd welcome some attention'. Hand-biting means, 'Give me attention! I'm lonely or bored'.

Behaviour that challenges exists in the space between the person and those who support them. To understand and address behaviour that challenges we have to get to know the person in order to provide the kind of support they need for us to deliver both a good quality of life and increased choice and learning.

Supporting individuals in a person-centred way is not for the faint hearted, the under-supported, or the indifferent. Person-centred support is provided by knowledgeable and passionate people. It takes commitment to work in the tensions between the demands of the team and the demands of doing what is right by the person.

Taking Amal's behaviour as communication means the team craft two key documents to help them support her in a more person-centred manner. An interaction profile sets out how the team promise to support Amal with her morning routine, as well as how to engage her in regular low-demand and fun activities. The team knows Amal prefers some staff to others, and the profile describes how to develop rapport with Amal. The document sets out the need to respond to screaming rather than wait for the more serious hand-biting. Crucially, it also describes a strategy to ensure Amal sleeps well: this involves 'quiet' time from 9pm, a warm bath, subdued instrumental music, and a hand massage. Amal enjoys a snack before bed. A V-shaped pillow helps her settle comfortably, as does a golden night-light. If Amal is relaxed, she sleeps better, and sleeping better means Amal is less tired come morning, more able to listen to staff, and less anxious.

The second document is a communication passport. This describes what methods of communication work best for Amal. Less talk and more signing seem to result in fewer problems but Amal also responds well to symbols, and she will point to symbols for certain foods and people. The team now use symbols and signs as their primary form of communication. The team ask a local speech therapist and psychologist to work with them to verify their discoveries and to offer them further advice.

Person-centred support is an 'upstream solution': providing the kind of support that meets the expectations and needs of individuals may contribute to amending or avoiding situations that lead to behaviour that challenges. As such, person-centred support can act as an antecedent intervention.

For Amal, the team change how they ask her to be involved in activities, they focus on preferred activities, they embed less preferred activities in fun interactions, and they teach alternatives to screaming and hand biting that achieve the same outcomes. These changes help reduce behaviour that challenges.

Person-centred planning

Person-centred planning is the foundation upon which a meaningful life can be crafted and tailored services delivered (Freeman *et al*, 2015). Using such approaches clearly demonstrates that service organisations are committed to taking people seriously. Being person-centred is not optional: it is the job.

It involves regular ongoing meetings to discover and describe what support the person requires to achieve what they want to achieve. Often services are built on our ideas of what suits people without bothering to tailor such places to individuals.

If it is true that regardless of our good intentions 'we cannot represent others in any other terms than our own' (Van Maanen, 1988), perhaps it is useful to gather the insights of others about what might serve the person best. Person-centred planning is a collaboration: people work in partnership to describe what they know. Families and friends are experts through experience and their insights about what people need to be supported well don't necessarily rely on busy professionals. They can provide unique perspectives and stories. There are two outcomes of planning: better understanding and better support. The plan is not the outcome, but the springboard to deliver what the person needs. A plan is never finished: it grows as knowledge is gathered from supporting the person.

> The team know that supporting Amal well is only one element of good service: they need to establish what kind of future Amal might prefer. Having goals and things to look forward to is important for many, and given the sudden changes in Amal's life some certainty is felt to be vital for her well-being. The service organisation employ two people with good experience of person-centred planning. The aim of their work is to describe a desirable future for Amal. This will help Amal's social worker and family think about what happens next.
>
> The team arrange a series of meetings between family members, Amal's social worker, and one of her ex-personal assistants. With Amal present, they describe what good support looks like for Amal, and they sketch out desirable futures. Amal contributes by signing, smiling, and selecting symbols but also through others having learned what matters to her. For Amal, any future involves being close to home, to the places and people she knows. Amal's team contribute their perspectives: Amal enjoys being busy, going to new places whilst enjoying familiar locations, trying new activities and meeting new people. Food is important to Amal (she loves to cook) as is predictability and people keeping their promises. Any future arrangement should encompass these attributes.

Plans can include descriptions of:

- the methods of communication the individual uses
- the living arrangements preferred by the person
- how the person prefers to be supported
- the activities and community spaces the person enjoys
- goals and hopes for the future.

A number of different planning methods exist and the one we use depends on whether we are seeking to understand how better to support someone now, or whether we wish to discover a desirable future. Most plans use more graphics and fewer words and they often describe how to support people to get to where they want to be, and how they wish to live (Sanderson *et al*, 1997).

Delivering a good quality of life is not simply an aspiration or outcome, but an intervention in itself. Tomorrow never comes for too many people whose behaviour challenges others, and many are expected to wait for their behaviour to ameliorate prior to receiving the opportunities that are their right. Quality of life seldom spontaneously occurs, and people with intellectual and developmental disabilities usually rely on the work of others to enable daily things others take for granted. Support needs to be well-organised and well-led in order for it to be person-centred.

Choice

A good quality of life is a subjective experience. Individuals value different things. But quality of life might be said to be the experience of a rewarding, enjoyable life surrounded by a rich network people we like. Did the support you provided people this morning or this afternoon deliver the same?

Most experts agree that self-determination (control and choice, making decisions, preferences expressed and respected by others) is an important part of a good quality of life (Schalock & Verdugo, 2002). There is evidence that shows that offering choices to people lessens behaviour that challenges (Carter, 2001), making it 'irrelevant, inefficient, and ineffective' (Carr *et al*, 2002, p.5).

Amal now has her first person-centred plan. The respite service is using elements of the plan – along with the interaction profile and communication passport – to inform their support of Amal; it tells them how to work and what to measure to show success. They now record not only the rate and duration of behaviour that challenges, but also the rate and duration of happiness and enjoyment. One of the important predictors of behaviour that challenges is Amal not having her choices respected: the team measure the number and type of choices Amal is offered and makes, to capture information about what she prefers.

Having choice is important for people. Choices can be small yet significant for happiness (for example, the sort of food we want, the activities we enjoy), or choices can be large (for example, where we live, with whom, how we are supported). In the UK the law assumes capacity exists to make choices and that what matters is not making the *right* choice but *their* choice. Some decisions are more demanding than others, however choices become more informed the greater our experiences of the options and outcomes.

Happiness

Amal's story consists not only of descriptions about how to support her, or respect her wishes, or enable her to be active; her story includes knowing the things she values, the people she loves, the difficulties she faces as a human being, and what she needs to be happy. Amal's story is happy and heart breaking but not uncommon. Services and professionals often collect paperwork, not stories, and so only catch a glimpse of the people they serve.

> Amal is well supported by a team of people who enjoy being with her. There's evidence of good rapport, communication is consistent, and Amal is enjoying her life: behaviour that challenges has significantly reduced by improving the quality of life experienced by Amal. The weeks turn into months, then a year: it takes time for Amal to develop positive relationships and trust. Amal's family are happy, too: they want Amal to live in her own place.
>
> After thirteen months, the team is saddened when told Amal will be leaving in a matter of weeks. Her social worker has found a service near her family. The respite team are fearful the new service doesn't make mention of Amal's person-centred plan. But they have collected a huge amount of information and knowledge concerning how best to support Amal and how to listen to her: they have accrued an understanding of her story. The team will pass this on, hoping others will also pay attention and listen to Amal.

When inducting new staff, positive stories should balance war stories. Many individuals have plans written about them that ensure staff keep them safe during incidents of behaviour that challenges. Far fewer have plans that describe how to ensure happiness is maintained, choice is not withdrawn and ruptured relationships are mended. Services keep antecedent-behaviour-consequence (ABC) records for behaviour that challenges, when they might also keep ABC records for appropriate behaviour or happiness. Happiness is a goal people can relate to and should be an accomplishment of support (Carr, 2007).

The previously mentioned methods – person-centred planning, person-centred support – can contribute to the inclusion of the voices of people using services. Such approaches can shape our understanding of what the person needs to avoid or amend predictors of behaviour that challenges, and they can give us insights into bigger issues they are facing.

People may live in a place and still not belong. Belonging comes from being active in a place, being valued in a place, and enjoying time there. Happiness and belonging are as valid as any other factor contributing to quality of life, and yet they are often seen as of secondary importance in 'managing' behaviour that challenges. It might be that working to deliver happiness and belonging contributes to reducing behaviour that challenges.

Implications

At the heart of our work to understand and respond constructively to behaviour that challenges is the requirement to work in a manner that delivers person-centred interventions. Including those too often excluded who have learned the only way to get others to listen is to hurt themselves or others, takes time and imagination. In the past services operated as if the people using them were passive recipients rather than active partners. People with intellectual disabilities are people to be understood, not puzzles to be solved; they are not square pegs to be forced into round holes others have carved.

Some people can tell us very clearly what they like and what they don't. Some people take a while to trust us. Some people show us what they like through their reactions to our work. Some people inform us through their behaviour that challenges. All these are hard to hear when we don't believe the person can tell us anything of value. Our attitude can act as a barrier to hearing what people are communicating.

Behaviour that challenges speaks of important things, but the absence of a thing can tell us as much as its presence: when behaviour that challenges reduces, the message seems to be, *'I'm living the life I like'*.

Key learning points

- How we think about people influences how we work with them.

- Thinking of behaviour that challenges as a form of communication means we spend time trying to understand the message.

- Person-centred planning refers to a number of methods of gathering information about who the person is, how they prefer to be supported, and their future aspirations; a plan describes how to support people better.

- Person-centred planning should involve as wide a range of people as possible, including the person, their friends and family, and people who know the person well.

- We can include people in decisions by asking them, by considering their responses to our support, and paying attention to their choices.

References

Carr EG (2007) The expanding vision of positive behaviour support: research perspectives on happiness, helpfulness, hopefulness. *Journal of Positive Behaviour Interventions* **9** (1) 3–14.

Carr EG, Dunlap G, Horner RH, Koegel RL, Turnball A, Sailor W, Anderson JL, Albin RW, Koegel LK, Fox L (2002) Positive behaviour support: evolution of an applied science. *Journal of Positive Behaviour Interventions* **4** (1) 4–16.

Carter CM (2001) Using choice with game play to increase language skills and interactive behaviours in children with autism. *Journal of Positive Behaviour Interventions* **3** (3) 131–151.

Ephraim G (1998) Exotic communication, conversations, and scripts – or tales of the pained, the unheard and the unloved. In D. Hewitt (Ed.) *Challenging Behaviour: Principles & practice.* London: David Fulton Publishers.

Freeman R, Enyart M, Schmitz K, Kimbrough P, Matthews K & Newcomer L (2015) Integrating and building on best-practice in person-centred planning, wraparound, and positive behaviour support to enhance quality of life. In: F Brown, JL Anderson & RL De Pry (Eds) (2015) *Individual Positive Behaviour Supports: A standards-based guide to practices in schools and community settings* (pp241-257). Baltimore: Paul H Brookes.

Pitonyak D (2005) *Jumping into the Chaos of Things* [online]. Available at: http://dimagine.com/wp-content/uploads/2018/03/Jumping.pdf (Accessed February 2019).

Sanderson H, Kennedy J, Ritchie P, Goodwin G (1997) *People, Plans & Possibilities: Exploring person centred planning.* Edinburgh: SHS.

Schalock R & Verdugo MA (2002) *Handbook on Quality of Life for Human Service Practitioners.* Washington: AAMR.

Van Maanen J (1988) *Tales of the Field: On writing ethnography.* London: University of Chicago Press.

Part 2: Gaining a Better Understanding

The following chapters are all about trying to understand the messages underpinning behaviour that challenges. Whilst exploring the reasons behaviour that challenges happens may require an assessment, there are often some fundamental issues we need to consider, such as communication, well-being, health and quality of life. Knowing the contexts to behaviour that challenges is vital to our understanding, and the foundation for beginning to craft not only good but *great* support.

Chapter 6: Assessing behaviour that challenges

By Lawrence Patterson & Jenna Szymanski

Summary

Behaviour that challenges can usually be understood with careful observations and by taking time to know the person and their environment and how these match. Forming opinions, and sharing these in a behaviour formulation based on what we find out, is helpful. Often it is possible to make some changes to the support plan that allows the person to have improved quality of life. If these changes do not help, or the risk is too high, then professional assessment may be required. Direct carers and supporters play a key role in assessing behaviours.

Although assessment may be seen as a professional task, the term assessment can be defined as a formal way of making an opinion about something. Carrying out assessment is important because human nature means that the opinions people have directly affect the way they act. This matters when trying to understand behaviour that is difficult or challenging. Behaviour is usually understandable when we look into the factors that could be causing it. There could be a combination of reasons for a person's actions. If we want to help positively influence people's lives we need to look for these reasons carefully. This could be done in the following ways:

Observe and describe

You may be thinking about a certain incident of behaviour and wondering what happened, or you could be thinking about a pattern of behaviour that a person shows over time. When trying to understand the reasons why someone has behaved in a certain way it is important to look carefully at both the person and their environment and try to describe the way that they are matched together. Think about what could be going on within that person (individual) and what is going on around that person (the environment) and how the two interact.

Figure 1: The interaction between the person and their environment and their behaviour

The following case study will help you to consider the kind of factors to look for and how to describe them:

Case study: Charlotte

Charlotte is a 46 year-old woman with a moderate learning disability. Charlotte lived abroad as a child and then moved to the UK at the age of 19 years. Charlotte enjoys listening to music, watching Jeremy Kyle, shopping and doing crafts. Charlotte can use speech but articulation and speed of delivery can be a challenge for her. Charlotte has a very dry sense of humour.

Charlotte moved into a residential placement for individuals with mild/moderate learning disabilities. Charlotte and the other people she lived with could mobilise independently, could complete most parts of their personal care independently or with little support, and could attend to daily cooking and cleaning tasks with little support. She resided there for 20 years. At the beginning of her time living at the residential service Charlotte showed behaviour that challenged which included swearing and shouting at staff, sometimes refusing medication and on occasion hitting out at staff. The service was in the south of England whilst her family lived in the midlands. Charlotte reportedly felt 'abandoned' by her family at this time. Charlotte's mother and father have since passed away but Charlotte does have a younger sister who lives in Scotland, Charlotte has a photograph of her on her wall but has very little contact with her.

In 2014 Charlotte's physical health deteriorated significantly and she was admitted to hospital. The episode of ill health resulted in substantial weight loss, the loss of the ability to walk independently and impaired speech. During her hospital stay and in the months after discharge her physical health began to improve but did not return to baseline. Whilst admitted to hospital it was decided that Charlotte's placement of 20 years was no longer suitable for her changing needs and alternative accommodation was sought; Charlotte was discharged to a new placement and never returned to her previous home. The new placement was set up to support individuals with more profound learning disabilities and mobility difficulties. It was thought to be appropriate as Charlotte now required a wheelchair, hoisting and increased hands-on support to mobilise safely.

Since Charlotte's episode of ill health and her move to new accommodation, Charlotte has displayed unusual types of behaviour that challenges that has increased in severity. From the day Charlotte moved into her new accommodation Charlotte began refusing to bathe, scratching and biting staff when they attempted to support her with personal care, swearing and shouting at staff when they entered her bedroom, directing verbal threats at other service users, frequently refusing medication and spending the majority of her day in bed. The staff team report that they are fearful of Charlotte and are often leaving her in her bedroom because they don't know how to help her without getting hurt.

Before you read on, think about the following questions:

- **What personal characteristics about Charlotte could be factors causing her behaviours?**

  - How does her learning disability affect her?

- What about other disabilities?
- What is important to her and is it missing from her life i.e. family contact, friends, social events, routine etc.

- **What environmental factors could be causing her behaviours?**
  - How does the home setting match her personal characteristics?
  - Would the level of activity suit her personal characteristics?

Table 1 below shows one way of noting down the factors related to Charlotte's behaviour that challenges.

Table 1

Individual	Behaviour	Environment
Moderate learning disability.	Refusing to bathe.	Moved to a new home setting.
Feeling of abandonment (by family) as a young adult.	Scratching staff when supporting with personal care.	Living with people who have more profound learning disabilities.
Parents have passed away.	Biting staff supporting her with personal care.	Never returned to previous home of 20 years.
Little contact with sister.	Directing verbal threats at service users.	Does not know the service users or staff at her new home.
Dry sense of humour.	Swearing and shouting at staff when they enter her bedroom.	
Enjoys music, crafts and watching Jeremy Kyle.	Refusing medication.	
Can use speech but is slow and can struggle to articulate herself well.	Spending lots of time in bed.	
Weight loss.		
Loss of independence.		
Loss of mobility.		

Getting to know the person

When thinking about behaviour we need to consider everything that could be part of the person's story. When thinking about the person and their behaviour there are several important characteristics to think about:

Communication

What is their understanding of the world around them? Do they need people around them to use sign language, do they need information to be written down and accompanied by pictures, can they understand changes in others' body language and facial expressions? And how do they make themselves understood? Spoken word, signs, gestures, taking you to something/somewhere etc.

Thinking point: Reflect on a time when you have not been able to get your point across or have not understood what is being asked of you.

Personal history

People receiving care and support sometimes have personal history that is not well understood. Family members can be a source of helpful information about behaviour the person displays. We must also consider the understanding the person has about their family, and the way that they are supported to have contact when this is possible. Check that the person consents to you speaking to their family wherever possible.

Tips: Ask family members or past carers about the person's behaviour in the past:
- Try to find out if anything helped the person that the family used to do.
- Be honest about any difficulties in helping the person have contact with their family. Try to come up with solutions together.

Physical health

Very often when people with learning disability or autism are displaying behaviour that is challenging it can be better understood when we consider their internal or physical state. Do they have an unmet health need, for example period pain, back ache, headache, constipation or toothache?

Thinking point: Consider a time when you have experienced toothache. Try to remember how it made you feel and how your behaviour changed.

- What health problems could be affecting the person's behaviour?
- Do they seem to have more energy at certain times?
- Are they sleeping well or having problems with sleep?
- How do they seem to be feeling within themselves?

Whenever any of these health factors are known to be part of the problem, be sure to involve a qualified health professional such as the GP or community nurse.

Is their environment a positive influence?

People are naturally shaped by their environment. For people with intellectual disability or autism it is especially important to have a good look at what is happening around them on a regular basis. When looking at the person's environment, some suggested aspects to think about are:

- The physical spaces and the potential impact of these on their behaviour (for example narrow corridors or doors that are sometimes locked).

- How the person appears to behave when around other people, perhaps other people receiving care and support.

- Are there aspects of the way the service is run that affect their behaviour (such as shift handover times)?

- How do they seem to behave when certain activities are happening or offered to them?

- Could the way that you and your colleagues respond to the person lead to them learning about behaviour in a way that is unhelpful?

By taking an objective look at the places where the person spends their time, it is possible to start to consider how well these settings match their personal needs.

Physical setting

Do they like clutter or minimalism? Do they like noise or peace and quiet? Do they like light or dark environments?

Thinking point: Consider your preferences; if you are a person who enjoys a quiet home, imagine living with someone who plays their music loud or a staff member who has a loud and booming voice.

Activities/occupation

Do they have enough to do? Are the activities enjoyable? Do they have choice over what they do, when they do it and who with?

Thinking point: How would you behave if you did not have enough to do each day or did not get to choose your activities?

People

Think about the people the individual is living with. Have people moved in or out? Are others displaying behaviour that challenges? Are the characteristics of the other tenants agreeable or disagreeable to the individual? Think about the people who support the individual. Do they have the required skills to work with them? Are they consistent or are there lots of staff changes? Are staff's characteristics agreeable or disagreeable to the individual?

Although it can feel uncomfortable to look at the way that we work and consider if it is adding to the person's difficult behaviour, it is one of the most important parts of assessing behaviour.

Reflecting conversations with colleagues, perhaps with support to facilitate by someone independent, can be extremely useful as a way to understand how there are differences between responses to the person and how they are supported to cope with stressful activities.

Whenever problems with the environment can be seen to be part of the issue be sure to involve the service manager, and potentially the responsible funding authority, to discuss how to adjust the person's environment to create a better fit for them. Again, if the person has family who are available and involved in their life, it can be extremely helpful to seek their views on how the environment could be best adjusted.

Formulation

Through conversations with others that know the person well, the next step is to write down some suggestions about what is happening and why. This is often called a behaviour formulation.

A behaviour formulation should include:

1. **A description of the behaviour** – try to steer away from describing the behaviour as an emotion e.g. 'they were angry' and try not to be too vague e.g. 'they hit someone'. Instead state clearly what you see.

2. **What led to the behaviour occurring** – refer to events that occurred before the problem behaviour. Include events in the person's recent past and also immediately before the behaviour.

3. **In basic terms say what you think the purpose of the behaviour is** – think about whether the person is seeking to gain something, e.g. attention, or stimulation, or whether they are seeking to avoid something.

4. **What do you think is reinforcing the behaviour** – think about what responses and/or consequences the behaviour provokes and whether the responses make the behaviour more or less likely to occur again.

Activity: Use the case study to practice writing a formulation, then have a look at this example formulation.

Example formulation

'Charlotte seeks to avoid interaction with staff by shouting, threatening, scratching and biting them when they enter her bedroom. This has resulted in Charlotte not washing, not taking medication and staying in bed all day. In response to Charlotte presenting with behaviour that challenges, staff are sometimes avoiding her which makes it more likely the behaviours that challenge will occur again. Charlotte was previously able to do most day-to-day tasks with little or no support so Charlotte is potentially frustrated at her loss of independence. Charlotte has only just moved to this home and so does not have a strong relationship with the staff, which is likely to make it even more difficult to receive support, particularly support with intimate tasks. This quick move may also have led to Charlotte experiencing a sense of →

loss/grief for her previous long stay placement, staff and housemates. Charlotte struggles to articulate herself well, her speech is slow and her communication has become further impaired since her illness. This may be contributing to the increase in Charlotte's presentation of behaviour that challenges.'

Make some changes in a shared behaviour support plan

Once a formulation is written down, check that other people think that it is a fair and representative explanation for the behaviour. You may need to check with family and other carers that they agree with your opinions or theories about why you think the behaviours are occurring and the strategies you want to put in place to try and improve the person's situation. This will involve making some planned changes to the individual's support plans to address the factors that are contributing to the behaviour.

Activity: Write a list of theories or opinions identified within your formulation and explain how you could make changes to the support plan. Then look at what you have come up with.

Theory: Charlotte is struggling with her loss of independence since her decline in health and mobility.

Possible changes: Staff might think about how Charlotte can make choices about her day and to do as much as possible for herself. Some possible changes: 1) staff might ask Charlotte whether she prefers to bathe in the morning or the evening, 2) identify the tasks or part of the tasks Charlotte can do unsupported so that she does not feel entirely dependent on others.

Theory: Charlotte is feeling a sense of abandonment as a result of moving on from a long term placement without being able to say goodbye.

Possible changes: Staff might ask Charlotte if she wants to have contact with her previous placement and facilitate this.

Theory: Charlotte's reduced ability to verbally communicate as a result of her further impaired speech.

Possible changes: Staff could think about limiting the amount of words Charlotte may need to give in response by asking yes/no questions or by giving a few choices e.g. showing her two CDs and asking which she would like to listen to. Staff could ensure they give Charlotte plenty of time to respond.

Once the adjusted plan is in place it is essential to regularly check with the individual to see how the new strategies affect their behaviour and quality of life. Aim to review the effect of changes in approximately two weeks' time. This will give you all an opportunity to reflect on whether the changes to the support plan have had a positive impact on the individual, whether further changes need to be made, whether you need to test for longer or whether you need further professional assessment.

When to seek further professional assessment?

Behaviour that challenges can pose significant risks and may not be positively impacted by making changes to the behaviour support plan within the service. Whenever a person's behaviour is placing them or others at significant risk of harm it is very important to request professional assessment and support. It is not always enough to create a detailed understanding of the person and their environment; there may be situations when seeking advice from the GP, community nurse or social worker will be important.

When the person's behaviour continues to be challenging even though you have addressed what you have seen to be part of their problem, it is always the right thing to request further functional assessment from a qualified professional. This is usually achieved with a referral to a specialist service, although the specialist professionals may also work in your same organisation.

How does the professional assess behaviour?

Whenever a professional is carrying out a behaviour assessment, they will be using tools and approaches to consider the function of the person's behaviour. Human behaviour has been shown to be most likely to be trying to achieve any one of the following functions:

- A sensory or stimulation sensation that may be pleasant or calming.

- To escape or avoid something that is experienced as unpleasant.

- A way of involving other people and feeling attended to, such as other people paying you attention.

- To work towards getting specific things and items that are needed or wanted.

Through detailed collection of information the professional will attempt to work out the functions of the person's behaviour that challenges. To do this they will rely on descriptions from direct carers, which may come from interviews or through writing down notes. A common way that these notes are written is in the format of an A-B-C record (sometimes called 'behaviour observation charts').

- **A** stands for '**Antecedent**' meaning any events before the behaviour of concern.
- **B** is the area on the record to describe the **Behaviour** in detail.

- **C** stands for **Consequence** and means the way that the behaviour was responded to.

If you are unsure about the way the professional assessment is being completed, be sure to ask for advice and if necessary bring the professional's attention to the understanding formed within the service of the person's behaviour that challenges, and successful ways to help them.

What strengths does the person have?

It is important to avoid sending only negative messages about people due to their behaviour. Whilst professional involvement is usually considered in the person's best interests, it can have a negative stigmatising effect on them, meaning they are seen negatively or just as a problem.

Be sure to highlight within any professional assessment the person's strengths. These could be:

- Individual skills and abilities they have that are important not to lose.
- People they see who they are supported well by, for example family and friends.
- Times and places when their behaviour is not challenging.

Sometimes the most important aspects of understanding a person's difficult behaviour can be found in understanding the times and places that they do not displaying behaviour that challenges at all. This is because human nature is to adapt to our surroundings and in some parts of their life the person may have found a much better 'fit' for themselves than in others. This can be an important source of information about how to positively influence their whole life.

Key learning points

- The interaction between the person and their environment is where to look for reasons for behaviour that challenges.
- Consider the person's internal needs and characteristics.
- Consider the environment the person experiences and reflect on how we support them.
- Write out a behaviour formulation and share it to help develop understanding of the person's behaviour.
- Where it is safe to do so, make some adjustments to the behaviour support plan based on the formulation.
- Professional assessment relies on direct carers' involvement. Try to ensure information is used fairly and accurately.

Further reading

NICE (2015) *Challenging Behaviour and Learning Disabilities: Prevention and interventions for people with learning disabilities whose behaviour challenges* [online]. Available at: https://www.nice.org.uk/guidance/ng11 (accessed February 2019).

Royal College of Psychiatrists (2007) *Challenging Behaviour: A unified approach* [online]. Royal College of Psychiatrists, British Psychological Society and Royal College of Speech and Language Therapists. Available at: https://www.rcpsych.ac.uk/docs/default-source/improving-care/better-mh-policy/college-reports/college-report-cr144.pdf?sfvrsn=73e437e8_2 (accessed February 2019).

Chapter 7: Communication and behaviour that challenges

By Jill Bradshaw

Summary

Communication is a key area in understanding not only why behaviour that challenges occurs, but also how we can try to prevent it happening in the future. Most people with intellectual and developmental disabilities have difficulty communicating. This includes being able to understand what other people are communicating and being able to express themselves. We also know from research that behaviours that challenges are more likely to be present when people have intellectual and developmental disabilities and significant challenges in being able to communicate (Bowring *et al*, 2017).

Why is communication so important?

The following case study will help you to consider ways in which communication difficulties may have led to behaviour that challenges.

Case study: Winston

Winston is a 40-year-old man with severe learning disabilities. He lives at home with his parents and attends a local day centre five days a week. Winston enjoys being outside and playing sports. He particularly likes football. He also enjoys spending time with members of staff. Winston's behaviours that challenge include hitting, kicking and biting people. These behaviours typically occur four or five times a week, almost always at the day centre, during times when Winston is left with little to do. The team have assessed Winston and think that Winston's behaviours serve the functions of access to staff attention and access to preferred activities. After an incident Winston is often taken outside by a member of staff who has a particularly good relationship with him, to play football. Staff at the day centre think that this is a good way for Winston to get rid of some of his energy.

Winston communicates using short phrases of one or two words. He also knows some signs but doesn't often use these unless he is prompted by other people. He is able to understand simple sentences. He has good understanding of words that relate to people, places or events (for example, names of people, shops, swimming etc). He understands when people talk to him about what is happening, or what he is going to do now. He has much more difficulty in understanding when the staff talk about →

things that are (or in this example, are not) going to happen in the future. Winston also has difficulty understanding words which relate to emotions, negatives (for example, not) and time concepts (for example, tomorrow). For example, if staff

say 'Winston, we are not swimming tomorrow, so you don't need to bring your trunks' then Winston will probably only understand 'swimming' and think that he is going swimming. In his experience, the most likely outcome of someone talking to him about swimming is that they are about to take him swimming. He is able to understand photographs and these are sometimes used with him.

Yesterday there was an incident of behaviour that challenges. Winston had had a busy morning gardening and had come into the centre to eat something. He had finished his meal quite quickly and was waiting for the afternoon activity. Winston repeatedly approached different members of staff saying 'football'. This happened five or six times. The staff were all busy and so typically responded by saying 'not yet mate' or 'not at the moment Winston' or 'we'll play football later' or 'you've just been outside, you can't play yet'. Winston became more agitated and eventually kicked and hit a member of staff. They were not seriously hurt. A member of staff was able to calm Winston down by taking him outside to play football.

Before you read on, stop and think about the following question.

■ What communication factors do you think might have contributed to Winston's behaviour that challenges?

■ Winston was using the communication skills he has to ask to play football (by saying 'football') but his requests were not successful.

■ Winston probably didn't understand the staff when they told him that he couldn't play football yet. The staff used words like 'later', 'not', and 'can't', which Winston is not able to understand.

In this situation, Winston had used his communication skills to ask for what he wanted. As staff were not able to meet his request, Winston eventually became more and more frustrated and then displayed behaviour that challenges. This behaviour not only resulted in him getting his preferred activity, it also resulted in him spending time with staff. This makes it more likely that Winston will display behaviour that challenges the next time this situation occurs as he was successful in getting his needs met. This means he is learning that behaviour that challenges is more effective than communication in getting his needs met.

Common communication difficulties that may contribute to behaviour that challenges

Behaviour that challenges may occur for a variety of reasons. Communication difficulties also often contribute. Even when people have relatively good communication skills, strong emotions (such as fear, anger or frustration) are likely to have an impact on communication. In these situations, people will often have more difficulty listening, understanding and expressing themselves.

Difficulties understanding communication

People may not understand what they are being asked to do, or when they are being asked to do it. People may not know what is happening. This may be a particular issue in novel and unfamiliar situations. People may misunderstand and expect something different to happen. People may not be able to let you know that they haven't understood.

Difficulties with expressive communication

Behaviour that challenges is more likely to occur when people find it difficult to tell you what they need. People may not have the communication skills necessary to communicate their needs, express their feelings, make choices, and explain that they haven't understood what is expected of them. Some people, particularly people who have profound multiple intellectual disabilities, may have very inconsistent ways of communicating and it can be very difficult to be certain about what someone may be trying to communicate. You might have to rely on making a best guess, using your knowledge about the person and the situation.

What can be done to improve communication?

Improving communication can be effective in reducing behaviour that challenges. Before you read on, stop and think about the case study again.

- What communication strategies could the staff have used to help in this situation?

  - Staff could have used a visual timetable to explain to Winston when football was happening. This is something that would need to be developed over time.

  - Instead of telling Winston that he was not going to play football yet, they could have told him what was happening at the moment, for example, 'We're having lunch now'. Again, this could have been reinforced with the addition of photographs or signs. Even better, they could have offered Winston an alternative activity that he was able to do. This might require planning ahead and having activities readily available.

  - Everyone has different needs for attention at different times. As Winston clearly wanted to be with a member of staff at that time, it would have been better if a member of staff had spent time with Winston immediately, in response to his verbal request. While this is not always easy to achieve, the reality is that if staff don't spend the time with the person then, they will have to spend the time with the person later anyway, dealing with the behaviour that challenges.

Common communication interventions that may help to reduce behaviour that challenges

Many of the interventions around communication are no different from what makes a good communication environment in services in general. However, creating a good communication environment is even more important in services for people whose behaviour is described as challenging. Skilled communication partners will be able to support the person with disabilities to make the most of the communication skills they have. Try to think about where, when and with whom the person communicates best. How does this communication partner interact? What do they interact about? Is there anything you can learn from this?

General communication strategies include:

- Try to get the person's attention (for example, use their name before you start to speak, or if appropriate, use a touch cue).

- Use simple language.

- Try to give one piece of information at a time to allow the person time to process what you are saying (for example, say 'Craig, sit down' and wait for this to happen before giving the next instruction, instead of 'come and sit down now Craig, because your food will be here in a minute').

- Focus on what you want the person to do rather than on what you don't want them to do (for example, say 'walk' rather than 'don't run').

- Where possible, back-up spoken communication with additional visual means (for example, signs, symbols, photographs and objects); your local speech and language therapist will be able to advise you on what visual means are likely to be most helpful and on how these can be introduced.

- Focus communication on what is happening or what is just about to happen (talking about future events may be confusing for the person).

- Try to have a consistent approach to communication; where people have few or inconsistent methods of communication it can be very difficult if everyone interprets these signals in different ways.

- Share information and try to agree on an approach to communication; communication passports can be very helpful as these contain relevant information about the ways in which the person communicates and how to support communication.

- Try to respond positively to any attempts to communicate.

- Think about communicative alternatives to challenging behavior; this is known as functional communication training; communicative alternatives are ways that the person can request what they need, instead of engaging in behaviour that challenges, for example see Table 1.

■ Make sure that communication is more effective than behaviour that challenges.

Table 1: Functions of behaviour and alternative communication	
Possible function of behaviour	Example of possible alternative communication
To avoid difficult demands.	Teach person to hold up a card that says 'I need help'.
To gain attention.	Teach person to put their hand up.
To access a desired activity or object.	Teach person the Makaton sign for desired activity or object.

Additional things to consider

Of course, there are many other factors and strategies that you could use that do not just focus on communication. The most effective strategies will be those that include a multidisciplinary approach, and are worked out in collaboration with the support staff and with those who know the person well. Family carers and friends are likely to be experts by experience and should be included. People with intellectual and developmental disabilities may also be able to give you important information about their views, particularly when adapted approaches are used, for example Talking Mats®.

It is also important to think about all the different ways that the person with intellectual and developmental disabilities is able to communicate. When behaviours described as challenging occur, people with intellectual and developmental disabilities may need additional support to express their thoughts and feelings. You may need to be even more aware of changes in body language and facial expression. The person may need to rely on you to interpret their communication. It is important that you make communicating as easy as possible during such times. In order to reduce behaviour that challenges, you need to make sure that you respond to and reinforce any attempts to communicate.

Communication and person-centred active support

Many people with intellectual and developmental disabilities have little to do in their daily lives and receive few opportunities for interaction and communication. We know from research that having little to do is likely to be one factor that makes the development of behaviour that is described as challenging more likely. Approaches that increase meaningful engagement and also offer choice and control, such as person-centred active support, have been found to increase opportunities for communication and interaction. It is often easier for communication partners to interact with people they are supporting or spending time with in a way that is meaningful, during a real activity. This helps communication 'in the here and now' and also means that people have something to talk about. Creating more opportunities to communicate is really helpful as it enables people to build their skills in using their communication skills to successfully influence what happens to them in repeated opportunities throughout the day. Approaches such as person-centred active support are a good way of helping staff to develop the skills to 'bridge the communication gap' and to help staff to provide good communication support so that people are able to take part in communication, using the skills that they have.

Conclusion

- Find out as much as you can about the person's communication skills.

- Try to make sure that everyone has a consistent approach to communicating with the person.

- Make communication as easy as possible, particularly during times when behaviour that challenges is likely.

- Think about the function (for example, gaining attention, avoiding difficult demands) that the behaviour that challenges may have for the person. Does the person have any other ways of communication this?

References

Bowring DL, Totsika V, Hastings RP, Toogood S & Griffith GM (2017) Challenging behaviours in adults with an intellectual disability: a total population study and exploration of risk indices. *British Jounal Clinical Psychology* **56** 16-32.

Further reading

Bartlett C & Bunning K (1997) The importance of communication partnerships: a study to investigate the communicative exchanges between staff and adults with learning disabilities. *British Journal of Learning Disabilities* **25** 148–153.

Bradshaw J (1998) Assessing and intervening in the communication environment. *British Journal of Learning Disabilities* **26** 62–66.

Bradshaw J (2002) The management of challenging behaviour within a communication framework. In: A Budarham & A Hurd (Eds) *Management of Communication Needs of People with Learning Disability*. London: Whurr Publishers.

Bradshaw J, Gore NJ & Darvell C (2018) Supporting the direct involvement of students with disabilities in functional assessment through use of Talking Mats®. *Tizard Learning Disability Review* **23** (2) 111–116.

Bradshaw J, Beadle-Brown J and Beecham J et al. (2013) Quality of communication support for people with severe or profound intellectual disability and complex needs. *Communication Matters* **27** (3) 24–26.

Kevan F (2003) Challenging behaviour and communication difficulties. *British Journal of Learning Disabilities* **31** 75–80.

Millar S & Aitken S (2003) *Personal Communication Passports*. Edinburgh: University of Edinburgh CALL Centre.

https://www.challengingbehaviour.org.uk/about-us/understanding-behaviour/communication-sheet.html

https://www.unitedresponse.org.uk/communication-resource

Chapter 8: Conceptualising quality of life

By Julie Beadle-Brown

Quality of life has become an important concept in the measurement of outcomes, and therefore effectiveness of human services such as health and social care services. The concept of quality of life has been much debated over the years but it is generally accepted that it:

- Involves basic human needs being met (food, shelter, dignity and respect) and then experiencing what Schalock and Alonso (2002) referred to as 'life enrichers' or 'life enhancers' – such as personal development, choice and control, social relationships and inclusion.

- Encompasses both objective elements such as having meaningful things to do, having opportunities to develop skills and interests, having friends, having money, seeing family, taking part in community activities, accessing health care etc AND the individual's perceived satisfaction with these aspects, taking into account the importance of each element to the individual.

An international collaboration put forward a consensus on the eight domains of quality of life and researchers have suggested a range of indicators of quality of life (e.g. Schalock *et al*, 2002; Bigby *et al*, 2014). Table 1 identifies the eight domains and gives some indicators for each domain.

The quality of life domains are inter-related and intertwined. So for example if we look at the domain of emotional well-being (which can also be thought of as mental health), in order to achieve increased self-esteem one needs to be engaged in meaningful occupation, trying new things and experiencing success. As such emotional well-being and personal development are very closely linked. For emotional well-being to be good, a sense of belonging to a family, household or community (of varying shapes and sizes) and a sense of being valued are also critical. As such, emotional well-being, social relationships and social inclusion are interlinked. You also need to feel safe and free from pain, hunger, or any other type of discomfort – in this case physical well-being and emotional well-being are intrinsically linked. Respect and dignity and feeling in control of your life and what is happening to you brings self-determination and rights into the picture.

Table 1: Quality of life domains and some indicators of each domain

Domain	Indicator/example
Emotional well-being	Contentment, satisfaction, freedom from stress, self-esteem.
Physical well-being	Health, being able to do activities of daily living (mobility, self-care), physical activity.
Material well-being	Housing situation (including ownership), work status and environment and financial status (income, benefits), possessions.
Personal development	Education, personal competence, achieving, having success, being productive.
Self-determination	Personal control and autonomy, having goals and expectations for your own life, having some choices, and preferences (and having these respected).
Interpersonal relations	Positive interactions with others (friends, staff, work colleagues), relationships with family and friends, support (emotional, physical or financial), doing things (recreation) with other people.
Social inclusion	Being in and being part of the local community, including having a role or contributing to the community and accessing support and services in the community.
Rights	Human rights such as respect, dignity, equality, right to family etc. Legal rights such as citizenship (including voting, advocacy), accessibility, and due process.

It's a bit like the song… the ankle bone is connected to the leg bone, the leg bone is connected to the knee bone, the knee bone is connected to the thigh bone… and so on. You need the parts of your body to be connected in order to stand up and move. The same is true for quality of life – achieving at least a basic level across all domains is needed in order to achieve a good life, but achieving a good quality of life in one domain can help ensure a good quality of life in other domains. Research tells us that these domains work across many countries and cultures and apply to all of us – not just those with learning disabilities.

However, there will of course be variation in the indicators of quality of life which will be more or less important for different people. Within the domain of material well-being, for example, one person might be happy with just enough money to pay the bills, eat reasonably well and maybe afford one or two luxuries like a holiday or a new phone. For others, money will be more important and having the latest gadgets, phones, luxury holidays etc will motivate people to earn more money. This might be at the expense of some other elements such as wider interpersonal relationships as they are too busy working to build new relationships.

For some people social inclusion might be going to the football match with 60,000 other people. For others going rambling with four people from the local rambling club might be a much more pleasant and manageable idea! As such, once a basic level of quality of life is achieved, personal value, preference and choice features within each quality of life domain.

Quality of life and behaviour that challenges

One of the key indicators of lack of emotional well-being is behaviour that challenges… you will have read elsewhere in the book about the causes of behaviour that challenges. One important cause can be lack of stimulation – i.e. nothing to do, no opportunity to be meaningfully occupied, little interaction with others, etc. Another will be stress and feeling anxious, perhaps due to lack of predictability and consistency in the environment and support. This is particularly an issue for autistic people but is true for all of us.

In addition to linking to emotional well-being, lack of physical well-being itself can also result in behaviour that challenges. So, for example, if someone is in pain or discomfort for any reason this could be due to a serious health condition, but it could also be a much more mundane issue that is unrecognised and untreated – such as constipation, allergies, headache, toothache, issues with vision, earache, menstruation and so on. It is very common for such issues to be overlooked when people focus on the disability and attribute everything to this – this is what we sometimes hear referred to as 'diagnostic overshadowing' – 'Oh don't worry about that, that's just his autism'. Not having effective ways to communicate, and not being able to be in control, can lead to frustration and potentially behaviour that challenges. Add pain, discomfort or stress into the picture and behaviour that challenges becomes even more likely.

Behaviour that challenges also has a negative effect on quality of life. Generally, staff are less confident in supporting people who show behaviour that challenges and in particular trying new things and engaging in positive risk taking with them. Linked to this is the fact that people who show behaviour that challenges are more likely to experience restrictive environments and practices and reduced control. This can have a direct impact on people's physical and emotional well-being, but also results in fewer opportunities to be involved and in control, especially in activities and relationships out of the home. This has a negative impact on their opportunities for work, for community inclusion, for personal development, for interpersonal relationships and for contributing to society in a way that will gain respect from others. As poor quality of life is a contributing factor for behaviour that challenges, people end up in a vicious and never-ending cycle.

Figure 1: Summary of the vicious cycle of behaviour that challenges and quality of life

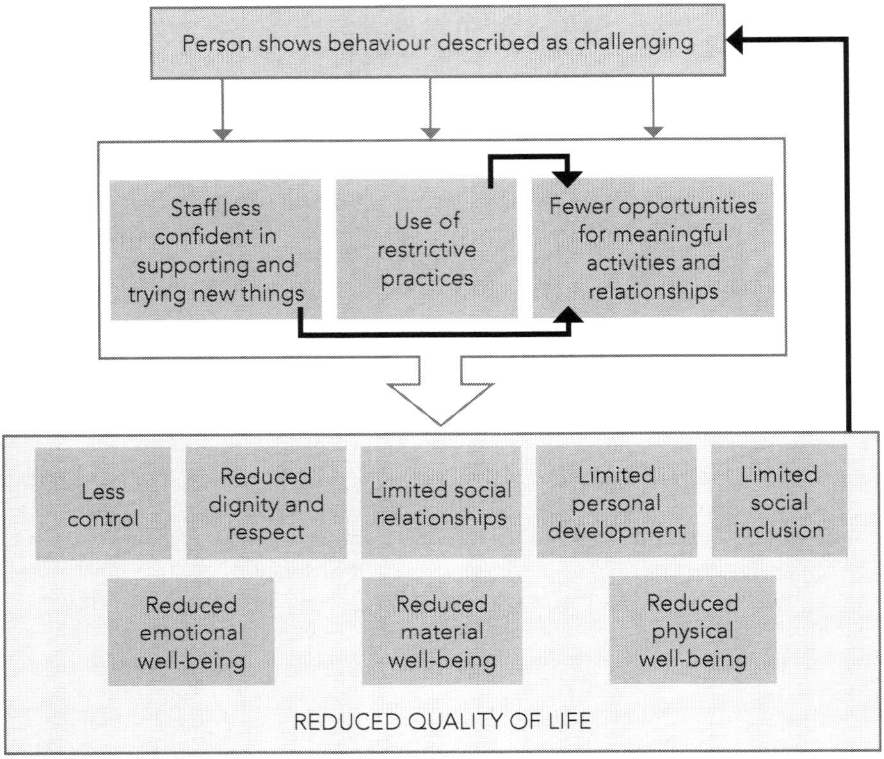

Case study: Michelle

Michelle is a young woman in her late 20s who arrived at her current service 18 months before I first met her. She had acquired the reputation of being one of the most challenging young women in the county. She had already had at least half a dozen placements and all of these had broken down. She was described as needing to sit behind a dog guard in the car so that she couldn't hurt the driver or cause an accident. The service was advised that she needed at least two staff with her at all times and that they needed to never say no to her and just give her whatever she asked for. Michelle was autistic and had a severe intellectual disability. She was considered to be generally non-verbal.

When staff from the service went to meet Michelle before agreeing her placement, they knew nothing about Michelle as a person. They did not know anything about her likes and dislikes, her skills, how she communicated. When they looked at her, their first conclusion was that she was miserable and had had absolutely no quality of life – no freedom, no control, no engagement, few relationships. They agreed to offer her a place and she moved in very quickly as her other placement had →

broken down. As a team, they agreed that the main priority was to first and foremost focus on gradually giving her a better quality of life and helping her to feel happy. Of course, they had to ensure they were prepared if she did show behaviour that challenges but they knew that if they focused on the quality of life rather than the behaviour that challenges they had a better chance of reducing the behaviour and of getting to know the real Michelle. As they supported her to have new opportunities, they began to learn much more about her. They quickly discovered that she could use Makaton in combination with understanding some key words and with support from the context and environment. They learnt that she loved her brother and motorbikes! She had picked up some more inappropriate habits over the years, but staff very positively and gently guided her towards more appropriate options. They discovered that she experienced a lot of pain in her feet, especially when she wore shoes, and that she was very unsteady when walking and needed physical support. She loved the smell of plastic aprons and bags and inflatable balls. She loved yoghurt (especially the black cherry one from M&S) and having tea in the café. She liked everything to be in the right place and was always putting away things that had been left in the wrong place.

They began to use this knowledge to extend her experiences further. Her love of plastic aprons, bags and balls was used to give her experience of accessing the community, making choices, handling money, meeting people. Initially she just went to the shop that sold the things she was interested in and went home but gradually more shops and the café were added on. She was allowed to bring the yoghurt she bought in M&S into the café and initially she would take her shoes off to give her feet a rest. She and her key worker would walk into town ensuring she had some exercise but afterwards she would have a foot spa to help her feet and would keep her shoes off at home. Overtime she began to get more involved in the tasks and activities around the home – setting the table, making drinks, putting away dishes (she was good at that part!). Although there was still always the possibility of behaviour that challenged in response to a sensory issue or frustration around communication (or even sometimes just to get attention) this had become much less frequent and much less severe. Staff had developed a way of asking her whether she could cope with different activities, e.g. going into particular shops, and she would respond. More and more she was signing 'yes'.

When I met her six months later, her life had changed immeasurably from where she had started – incidents of behaviour that challenged were few and far between. Her feet were better and she no longer needed to take her shoes off in public. She no longer needed to be asked whether she could cope in a shop before going in as she now really enjoyed this. She was now frequently smiling and engaged in a wide range of opportunities, had contact with her family and was starting to be able to cope better with other people around her, engaging in shared activities. She even attended the house disco, which would have been impossible for her six months previously.

How do we break the vicious cycle?

Well, essentially, we start pedalling backwards and focus on improving people's quality of life. Improving quality of life is a key part of reducing behaviour that challenges, and a central tenet of positive behaviour support – true to the cyclical idea (or perhaps a chicken and egg scenario is more appropriate), a better quality of life is both an intervention and an outcome of successful positive behaviour support. So how exactly do we improve people's quality of life?

The importance of engagement

Engagement in meaningful activity and relationships has been considered a particularly important element, in that it is the vehicle by which almost every aspects of quality of life are realised (Mansell & Beadle-Brown, 2012). None of the quality of life domains referred to in this chapter can be achieved if people are not actively involved in what is going on around them – e.g. you cannot become socially included if you don't take part in ordinary activities in the community; you can't make friends if you don't interact with other people or if you have nothing to interact about/over. If you are not physically active, you are less likely to experience good health. If you are not engaging in new activities successfully, then you cannot develop in self-esteem.

In addition, Mansell and Beadle-Brown (2012) argue that engagement is also an indicator of good quality of life – if people choose to be engaged then it is a sign of emotional well-being and a sign that the support for that person is working well. When they say 'yes' to an opportunity to engage, however that is expressed, they are saying that 1) they were offered something that was at least vaguely interesting, 2) it was done in a way that they understood what was being offered and what was required of them (at least to get started), and 3) that they had a history of successful support and therefore trusted that the person supporting them would give them enough support to ensure they succeeded. One of the first key indicators of changes in well-being (emotional and physical) is a change in how the person engages with their environment, including the people in it.

So what do we mean by engagement in meaningful activities and relationships?

Engagement is defined (see Mansell & Beadle-Brown, 2012) as actively participating in activities, tasks or interactions – this can be doing something constructive with materials, interacting with others or taking part in a group activity. Engagement can be doing the whole activity, task or interaction, or it can just be doing a small part of it. People might be able to do a large part of the activity, task or interaction independently, or they may be completely reliant on assistance from others to get engaged. 'Meaningful' in this context means that the activity, interaction or task in some way promotes the person's quality of life – e.g. it helps them to grow in skills/independence, experience real choice and control or become a more valued member of their community, accepted, respected, contributing.

What is needed to help people to become more engaged and therefore improve quality of life?

Although we know from research that living in small ordinary houses in the community is a necessary condition for a better quality of life, we also know that it is not sufficient (Mansell & Beadle-Brown, 2010; Bigby & Beadle-Brown, 2018). Even living in your own home with one-to-one support does not guarantee better quality of life outcomes. Although it is clear that person-centred planning and person-centred thinking can be very helpful for putting the person at the centre of their own lives and for ensuring regular review and a focus on further development of people's quality of life and achievement of their personal goals, there is no evidence that these alone support better quality of life overall. Likewise, individualised funding (e.g. personal budgets) should in principle give people more control over their lives, in particular over where they live, who they live with, who supports them, in what way. However, on its own, just having a personal budget is not enough to ensure a good quality of life.

What research has consistently found over the past 40 years is that only two things really matter – the severity of disability experienced by an individual and the nature of the support they receive (Mansell & Beadle-Brown, 2012; Bigby & Beadle-Brown, 2018). What makes the most difference is that the support received is enabling and empowering – i.e. that those providing support are assisting people to do as much as possible for themselves – doing 'with' not 'or' or 'to'. Over the years, this has become known as active support or person-centred active support (see Mansell & Beadle-Brown (2012) for a review). Person-centred active support is defined as 'providing just enough help and support to enable people to participate in meaningful activities and relationships so that people gain more control over their lives, gain more independence and skills and become a more valued part of their community, irrespective of the degree of intellectual disability or the presence of any additional conditions or needs' (Beadle-Brown *et al*, 2017; Mansell & Beadle-Brown, 2012). No one is too disabled, too autistic, too challenging, too epileptic, too ill to be more involved and have more control – however, the more severe the disability and the more complex the needs the more skilled the support needs to be. Person-centred active support is about recognising that everything that goes on at home, at school or college, at work, and in the community is an opportunity for people to participate, to gain new skills and experiences, to experience choice making and to meet new people. It is about providing people with many frequent opportunities to participate in new and familiar activities at a pace and intensity that works for them. It is about supporting people's understanding and supporting them to communicate their experiences, wishes, preferences. It is about providing just enough of the right help – not too much otherwise people will not learn or develop and not too little otherwise people will not be successful. Finally, it is about in all things respecting individuals as individuals and supporting them to have as much control over every aspect of their lives as possible. For people who show behaviour that challenges, the principles of 'little and often' and 'maximising choice and control' are particularly important – overcoming a history of failure is often required. Really important is the recognition that the most effective way of helping people develop skills is by giving them opportunities and the support to achieve. Recently, two experienced advocates and trainers in the field of disability rights (with lived experience of disability and neurodiversity), gave feedback after hearing about person-centred active support for the first time: 'For 30 years, the disability field has been working on the basis that we have to give people the skills in order to have opportunities, when we should have been focusing on giving people opportunities so that they could develop skills'.

Linked to the 'enabling relationship' is the development of a positive and helpful environment – an environment that is accessible, that promotes independence and control, that reduces anxiety and stress through structure that promotes predictability and consistency; an environment that is marked by positive approaches and expectations and is based on respect and understanding of each individual – i.e. empathy. This includes understanding their needs (those associated with their disability or mental health condition, those associated with health conditions, those associated with their history and previous experiences), understanding how they experience the world and understanding their skills and preferences. This understanding is important in identifying changes in people's physical and emotional well-being – especially when people have difficulty expressing how they feel through verbal communication. This understanding is also key in understanding why people might show behaviour that challenges. The best way (in fact probably the only reliable way) to develop this true understanding of individuals is through day-to-day experience of supporting them to try new things, to develop their skills, to meet people, to contribute to their community, to experience success, while observing their reactions to these opportunities.

References

Beadle-Brown J, Ashman B & Bradshaw J (2017) *Person-centred Active Support Training Pack (2nd edition)*. Brighton: Pavilion Publishing & Media.

Beadle-Brown J, Ashman B & Bradshaw J (2017) *Person-centred Active Support Self-study Guide (2nd edition)*. Brighton: Pavilion Publishing & Media.

Bigby C, Knox M, Beadle-Brown J & Bould E (2014) Identifying good group homes: qualitative indicators using a quality of life framework. *Intellectual and Developmental Disabilities* **52** (5) 348-366.

Bigby C & Beadle-Brown J (2018) Improving quality of life outcomes in supported accommodation for people with intellectual disability: what makes a difference? *Journal of Applied Research in Intellectual Disabilities* **31** (2) e182-e200.

Mansell J & Beadle-Brown J (2010) Deinstitutionalisation and community living: position statement of the Comparative Policy and Practice Special Interest Research Group of the International Association for the Scientific Study of Intellectual Disabilities. *Journal of Intellectual Disability Research* **54** (2) 104-112.

Mansell J & Beadle-Brown J (2012) *Active Support: Enabling and empowering people with intellectual disabilities*. London: Jessica Kingsley.

Schalock RL & Alonso MAV (2002) *Handbook on Quality of Life for Human Service Practitioners*. Washington, DC: American Association on Mental Retardation.

Schalock RL, Brown I, Brown R, Cummins RA, Felce D, Matikka, L, Keith KD & Parmenter T (2002) Conceptualization, measurement, and application of quality of life for persons with intellectual disabilities: report of an international panel of experts. *Mental Retardation* **40** (6) 457-470.

Further information

Person-centred support YouTube channel: https://www.youtube.com/channel/UCeeTvLnOkjRj5M6715orqdg.

United Response *Foundations of Good Support*: https://www.unitedresponse.org.uk/foundations-of-good-support.

United Response *Guide on Active Support*: https://www.unitedresponse.org.uk/active-support-guide.

Part 3: Delivering Support

These chapters are about putting into action the knowledge we've gained through our exploring and assessment. Having acquired an understanding of the message the behaviour that challenges seems to be sending, we now must respond. Any support should be based on a clear understanding of the purpose of the behaviour that challenges, and that support must be implemented in a way that ensures those who provide support are involved in the creation of strategies and are working well together. Thus this section contains advice concerning the vital importance of competent leadership, the need for rapport between people using services and those providing support, as well as how to organise the environment, teach new skills, and keep everyone safe.

Chapter 9: Practice leadership and behaviour that challenges

By Roy Deveau

I would like to acknowledge the help of Netta Goodban, Beverly Leahy and Tony Osgood for commenting on earlier drafts.

Summary

This chapter will show how good leadership helps grow great support. We often overlook the fact that those providing support have their own needs. If we want support staff to work well, they should be led well, offered training and development and involved in decisions. To set out how best to support staff, this chapter will show the origins of the ideas about practice leadership, the research supporting it, and what it looks like in practice.

Introducing practice leadership: past and current contexts

Mary[1] is a deputy service manager and is a great practice leader. She works in two houses working directly with staff and five individuals living in the houses. The people living there have a range of diagnoses including autism, intellectual disability and personality disorders. Serious behaviour that challenges happens every day. Mary often works directly alongside support workers, and when she's not doing so, often receives phone calls from staff asking for advice when a crisis occurs. Mary's service is the first service that has been able to support the residents to live out of hospital for long periods. Mary spends a lot of time trying to develop the staff team, who are caring but do not feel confident to 'do what she does'. One of Mary's other tasks is to produce the weekly service management report for the board of directors. These are always late or not done. Mary is now on a PIP (performance improvement plan) and if no improvement occurs Mary will be disciplined for failing to provide senior managers with weekly reports. Mary explained her role in supporting five of the most challenging people in the organisation and asked 'What do you want me to do leave the clients and staff to get on with it to do your reports, I can't do both'. Mary was told to get the reports done and manage her time better.

---

1 Mary is used throughout this chapter as a case study to present actual examples gathered from different sources over years.

In terms of managing services for people with learning disabilities, Mary is a practice leader, not an administrator. Her priorities are supporting staff and service users to get the best they can from life.

Practice leadership is a style of management used by front-line managers that is focused on supporting staff to constantly reflect upon and improve the support they provide.

It is particularly important in stressful and dynamic environments. It is all too easy for managers to become swamped by administrative duties, and to lose sight of their real value: using their experience and knowledge to help staff consider their interactions with those they support. Practice leaders show by doing, and manage by being present or available 'on the floor'.

The term practice leadership is associated with the 1970s in the UK when a group of academic practitioners were promoting ideas of an 'ordinary life' in ordinary community settings for all people with learning disabilities. They thought that even people with the most serious behaviour that challenges should have an ordinary life instead of living in isolated hospitals where 'patients' were subject to controlled, institutionalised routines.

One study of the 1970s looked at care of severely learning disabled children and contrasted hospital 'institutionalised' care and community-based, children's home 'child' focused care. They focused upon the role and performance of staff, in particular, the 'heads of unit'. The heads in children's homes spent more time working with children and were more 'accepting' and less 'rejecting' of children approaching them. Hospital unit heads spent more time in office administration and domestic work. The staff acted much as their respective unit heads did. The children, in homes, were observed to be more communicative and engaged in activities.

> *'Perhaps the most difficult part of the interventions* [placing people with behaviour that challenges in community homes] *was redefining the role of house managers and patch managers as primarily concerned with 'practice leadership' rather than administration.'*
> (Mansell *et al*, 1994)

Mansell and Elliott (2001) subsequently showed that administrative pressures upon managers are in turn transmitted to staff. Staff reported they expected 'consequences' from managers for not doing administrative tasks but were less certain of receiving consequences for undertaking 'enabling' work with service users.

This cuts to the heart of the continuing problem: what is the actual role of managers?

Staff experiences of behaviour described as challenging

A common finding in research is that supporting people whose behaviour challenges those around them is not easy. Staff have reported feeling tense, anxious, even sad and angry.

A culture of blame can easily develop: staff are blamed for behaviour that challenges, managers are blamed for not being present or understanding. All too easily a rigid focus on the person being responsible for their behaviour emerges. A good practice leader will identify early 'corrupted cultures' of care, such as those highlighted at Winterbourne View. Good practice leadership ensures staff remember their job is to deliver a good quality of life, not control behaviour.

The first government report on behaviour that challenges (Department of Health, 1993) noted exemplary services have staff and front-line managers who focus upon 'getting to know the individual'.

> 'The key to the difference between good and indifferent community services lies not in resources, but in the quality of management (especially first line management).'
> (Department of Health, 1993, p12)

Some research suggests it may not be experiencing behaviour that challenges itself that leads to negative experiences (and possibly poor or unhelpful practice) for staff. These negative experiences may result from poor 'organisational support' provided to staff. Staff experiences of behaviour that challenges are better if colleagues, and especially their immediate manager, are supportive. Deveau & McGill (2016a) have shown that effective practice leadership is associated with less staff stress and burnout, better teamwork and job satisfaction and trust in managers.

Developing rapport between staff and service users

Staff who can develop good positive relationships with people are 'getting to know the individual'. Some staff develop this rapport naturally; their 'instincts' lead them to develop good relationships and when they are on shifts less behaviour that challenges occurs. Some staff will need support and good practice leadership, like Mary provides. One study (McLaughlin & Carr, 2005) showed that staff with 'good rapport' were less likely to 'initiate' behaviour that challenges and were more likely to engage service users in activities. Three things helped some staff develop better rapport:

■ Coaching in 'non-contingent presentation of reinforcers' – staff providing everyday preferred activities, without these having to be earned by good behaviour.

- 'Responsivity training' – getting staff to respond to communication attempts by service users, don't ignore people or ask them to wait; 'ignore the behaviour not the person'.

- Coaching in 'turn taking' – staff give people time and space to respond, they don't keep talking, they listen.

Good practice leaders can use the above on-the-job coaching with staff in an informal way, or have it in staff development plans and collect data to check how it is working. Other research has focused upon mindfulness or emotional intelligence to support better staff/service user relationships. Empathy is important for staff managing behaviour that challenges and is part of emotional intelligence; being aware of and able to express and control one's emotions. Practice leaders will provide opportunities for staff to express how they feel in challenging situations and help to develop self-control.

Engaging service users in meaningful activities: active support and practice leadership

Supporting engagement in meaningful activities that people find enjoyable is key to ensuring a high quality of life and helps to prevent behaviour that challenges. Person-centred active support (PCAS) is one programme for supporting such engagement. Research is showing that practice leadership is key to how well PCAS is implemented.

Staff should experience the enabling presence of a practice leader. Staff will notice a practice leader watching them work and providing constructive feedback, modelling how best to support people, and solving problems in person-centred ways that improve quality of life. Team meetings and individual mentoring and supervision will be focused on reflecting on what works best to support people to successfully engage in activities.

Unfortunately, we also know that front-line managers do not appear to provide much practice leadership. Research in one large organisation showed the staff overall scoring their manager as providing just under half on a measure of practice leadership (Beadle-Brown *et al*, 2014). Other research showed that service managers find it difficult to provide on-the-job coaching, an essential element of PCAS training for staff (Jones *et al*, 2001). Mary says:

> *'Apart from all the administration managers have to do, very few service managers have any training in how to be a practice leader or providing on-the-job coaching.'*

Practice leadership in action

Throughout this book you will read statements e.g. 'staff need to be present' 'to communicate' 'to develop' 'to experiment' (see Osgood here). Just telling staff to deliver a behaviour support plan by saying 'read it from the file and sign it to say you understand it' will not help staff to work well with people who can challenge with confidence and consistency. This is a sign of a manager getting on with the paperwork and getting the reports in on time, unlike Mary. The following three areas will help and are based upon findings by Deveau & McGill (2016b).

Getting to know what staff and service users are really doing

Good practice leaders do not rely on records to tell them what is happening. They discover what is actually happening by being there observing and through discussions with staff and people using services.

Practitioners developing PCAS often use structured observations, ticking categories of staff activity (momentary time samples every 20 seconds). Many practice leaders feel these may be helpful but place more emphasis upon less structured 'realistic' observations, on being part of what is going on and hearing as much as seeing. Mary says:

> 'All the different tasks I have to do, my managers expect me to have all this paperwork done. They say it's kind of time management and I think some things are an absolute necessity, you have to do them. I think as a manager, you have to know what's going on, I have to know what's going on with all my clients in relation to their behaviour, their activity and their health. To me it's paramount that I know exactly what's going on in the home. The staff behave differently when the manager's around, I keep it informal, sit around and then you get to see how the staff actually behave towards the residents.'

Poor and maybe abusive practice can be hidden from managers who are not practice leaders (for example Winterbourne View). First reactions to difficult behaviours, by staff teams, even good ones, are often to remove things or stop people from doing things. For example, the kitchen gets locked because a kettle was thrown – people are denied scheduled activities or visits to places because staff are not sure how they may behave and so on. These immediate responses can very quickly become long term management strategies, for no good reason. They become informal aspects of the 'culture', expected and accepted ways of behaving.

Developing new ways to practice

Providing person-centred routines reliably and developing new opportunities is always of the greatest importance in services with good practice leadership. Good practice leaders do not develop care or behaviour support plans without staff being and feeling fully involved and included. In services with good practice leadership staff are always suggesting new, improved or different ways to practice.

Including staff experiences and their tacit knowledge in developing support strategies comes naturally to practice leaders. They know having staff on board with strategies they have contributed will support better plans and better implementation.

Mary says:

> 'Its important staff feel ownership of plans they have to work to, "singing from the same hymn sheet". No one person writes our care plans, again it's a collective thing and important for the staff team, and the service users of course, to feel they've got ownership of that particular care plan, otherwise it doesn't work. The worst thing was for a psychologist ... who'd be sitting in an office externally to write a care plan and produce it then ask you to run that. It's hijacked because staff feel that no-one understands how difficult this person is and of course we can't do that. We can sit in the office and come up with ideas, but the staff often have better ideas. Because they're always in the environment and they're the ones dealing with the behaviour that challenges, a little bit more than people up here making decisions.'

Managers who are focused on administration risk leaving things to chance, and whoever has the strongest voice in the staff team or a positive behaviour support (PBS) practitioner, who doesn't know the service or service user, can end up producing a PBS plan which won't work.

Good staff get to know the individual and how they like being supported by being with them often and being interested in them. This is called 'tacit' learning and is very important. Mary learnt this:

> ' ... a service user Paul needed a physical intervention to get him out of the door and into the community and we wanted to reduce our use of restrictive interventions. John from the PBS team and I did a lot of work with the staff team. But because we involved two staff who worked a lot with Paul they changed the whole guidelines from what John and I thought, into how they felt and they led training sessions with the staff team, and they did role play and showed the staff, whilst John and I are sitting there observing them doing it. Paul hasn't needed a physical intervention for months.'

Getting staff involved does not mean practice leaders give up management responsibility. Practice leaders like Mary know the work is not about their ego or status, but about delivering a high quality of life to those using services, and making the service a good place for staff to work. Mary says:

> 'If they've got a better way, explain it to me and if it works, it works and we'll do it your way. I've always been like that; I'm prepared to learn from the staff as well as to teach the staff.'

Using data

Mary is sceptical of PBS advisors or senior managers who want a lot of data collected; she is concerned that staff spend all their time recording data that nobody uses.

'We send all this data in but never see any results from it or see it back again.'

But Mary also knows that collecting and using data to inform how front-line staff work is vital.

As Deveau and Leitch (2018) say 'without data all we have is opinion' and the opinion of the 'strongest members of the team may well be negative, pointless or downright harmful'. Practice leaders use information from staff and their own observations.

To be useful data has to be accurate and detailed enough. It is important to collect data for a specific purpose e.g. to monitor response to a new programme for developing a skill or managing a challenge and reducing restrictive practice. When the skill is embedded the data collection can cease.

Working with a PBS practitioner, Mary said:

'I was fed up, staff being punched and blaming Bill, I could see it was often because they were not recognising or responding to Bill's attempts to communicate, especially in the kitchen during meal prep. I developed a simple observation form, three columns and watched staff with Bill for ten minutes whilst he and staff were preparing lunch. I described what happened in columns and many staff were very surprised at how bad they were at recognising and responding well to him. It really helped in changing how they interacted with Bill.'

Bill approached staff.	Staff responded positively.	Staff ignored or responded in a way which stopped his communication – consequence.
Bill made his usual noise when he tries to gain attention from staff, as he approached James in the kitchen.	James said 'I don't have time now Bill'.	James was punched on the cheek by Bill.

Developing staff and service users' skills abilities – shaping staff practice

Good practice leaders are focused upon developing skills and abilities of all the people in a service. They tend to be persistent with new staff, including those who show they want to learn but may find it difficult. Mary says:

> *'Some of the people* [I found] *were in a position that they didn't understand the role, the job, are still here today. Because they said, "I do want to do more", they've jumped on board ... we had some teething issues for all ... but these two have come through ... they now know how to do their job ... So I was right to try and support and develop people, rather than just say "we need you out".'*

Staff responding to challenges often have to act quickly in order to manage behaviour to prevent harm to people and prevent escalation to more serious behaviour. At these times staff may be feeling tense or anxious, annoyed, even angry – aroused by the need to act and think quickly. 'Thinking on your feet' (Ravoux *et al*, 2012) is how staff may describe it. At these tense times staff are also expected to remember many policy and legal obligations e.g. human rights, duty of care, least restrictive intervention and so on. Practice leaders need to support and shape staffs' behavioural responses through training and development to meld their personal instincts to the agreed plan.

Two things are necessary for such behavioural shaping – opportunity to **practice** and immediate **feedback** (Kahneman). This is the essence of competency training and central to the EDDY training described below. Practice leaders should create other opportunities for staff to shape their practice e.g. reflection on 'incidents', post-incident review at team meetings and discussion in individual supervision meetings.

> *'No, no* [I don't wait until supervisions to feed back things] *because I think you forget, so I keep running in here to write things down ... If I've seen something ... I might pass it on to the senior to bring up at their supervision. But I'm quite an impulsive person anyway so if I see something that shouldn't be happening I address it there and then.'*

One method for developing staffs' competence and confidence in providing detailed behavioural responses to service users e.g. for developing a skill (such as rapport) or presenting preventive (de-escalation) responses to help a service user calm down without presenting more serious challenges, is 'EDDY'. **E**xplain – **D**emonstrate – **D**o under supervision – **Y**ou have a go (see Deveau & Leitch (2018) for more detail). EDDY can be used by practice leaders either informally to remind them what staff would need to learn a new skill, or planned as an agreed staff development. Mary again:

> *'One of the guys we support has great difficulty getting up and going in the mornings. I am not the best at working with him but two of the staff are great. So I want to use EDDY and get these two to work out what and how they do so well, formulate this into a document or video role play. They can then be the practice leaders and take other staff through the EDDY stages. Make sure the staff understand that they watch these*

two demonstrate the programme, supervise them when they try it for themselves and be there for support once they have a go. I will keep an eye on it all and make sure it is recorded.'

Everybody's job: dispersed practice leadership

Service managers have largely been seen as responsible for providing practice leadership. Times have changed. Managers increasingly face being responsible for several services/homes in dispersed settings. Even when they want to act as practice leaders this will be very difficult. This means practice leaders will seek to develop other staff to provide practice leadership. Some organisations take this seriously and service managers see their role as 'distributing' and supporting practice leadership by other staff e.g. team leaders and senior support workers, and even key workers in the smallest, individualised homes.

References

Beadle-Brown J, Mansell J, Ashman B, Ockenden J, Iles R & Whelton B (2014) Practice leadership and active support in residential services for people with intellectual disabilities: an exploratory study. *Journal of Intellectual Disability Research* **58** (9) 838–850.

Department of Health (1993) *Services for People with Learning Disabilities and Challenging Behaviour or Mental Health Needs*. London: Department of Health.

Deveau R & Leitch S (2018) *Person Centred Restraint Reduction: Planning and action*. Birmingham, UK: BILD.

Deveau R & McGill P (2016a) Impact of practice leadership management style on staff experience in services for people with intellectual disability and challenging behaviour: a further examination and partial replication. *Research in Developmental Disabilities* **56** 160–164.

Deveau R & McGill P (2016b) Practice leadership at the front line in supporting people with intellectual disabilities and challenging behaviour: a qualitative study of registered managers of community-based, staffed group homes. *Journal of Applied Research in Intellectual Disabilities* **29** (3) 266–277.

Jones E, Felce D, Lowe K, Bowley C, Pagler J, Strong G, Gallagher B, Roper A & Kurowska K (2001) Evaluation of the dissemination of active support training and training trainers. *Journal of Applied Research in Intellectual Disabilities* **14** (2) 79–99.

Kahneman D (2012) *Thinking, Fast and Slow*. London: Penguin Random House.

Mansell J & Elliott T (2001) Staff members' prediction of consequences for their work in residential settings. *American Journal on Mental Retardation* **106** (5) 434–447.

Mansell J, Hughes H & McGill P (1994) Maintaining local residential placements. In: E Emerson, P McGill & Mansell J (Eds) *Severe Learning Disabilities and Challenging Behaviour: Designing high-quality services*. London: Chapman and Hall.

McLaughlin DM & Carr EG (2005) Quality of rapport as a setting event for problem behavior assessment and intervention. *Journal of Positive Behavior Interventions* **7** (2) 68–91.

Ravoux P, Baker P & Brown H (2012) Thinking on your feet: understanding the immediate responses of staff to adults who challenge intellectual disability services. *Journal of Applied Research in Intellectual Disabilities* **25** (3) 189–202.

Chapter 10: Building a good rapport

By Maria Hurman

Introduction

In this chapter we will consider the impact of having a good rapport between people with a learning disability and those that support this group of people. The chapter considers why rapport is important and how we feel when we are supported by others with whom we have a good rapport. Rapport is best understood when we put ourselves in the position of the person with a disability. For some individuals a good rapport with support staff can be effective in reducing behaviour described as challenging and the reasons for this are explained. A case study gives an example of a simple strategy for building rapport between Daisy who has a mild learning disability and Ron who supports her. The process of building rapport is described along with consideration of steps to take if rapport becomes damaged.

Key learning point

Having a good relationship with people being supported can in some circumstances bring about a reduction in behaviour described as challenging.

What is rapport and why is it important?

Have you ever wondered why some of the people you support will respond very differently to different members of staff in the same team, or to other people that they come into contact with? It could be that the person is asked to do something by one member of the team and either gives no response, refuses to comply with the request and on some occasions presents behaviour described as challenging. Another member of the team makes the same or a similar request and the individual happily complies or engages. Rapport or the quality of relationships that this individual has with different members of the same team may go some way to explaining what is happening here.

To define rapport the Oxford and Collins dictionaries use words like 'relationships' and 'communication' that are 'useful, harmonious, sympathetic or understanding'. In this chapter the term rapport is used to explain relationships; that the person with a learning disability may have with others, that are of a good quality, high in interpersonal warmth and connectedness.

Relationship quality is important in many fields of work and is noted as such in handbooks and practice guidance for professionals. If a doctor does not have a reasonable rapport with the patient they are treating, it is unlikely that the patient will communicate well, discuss their symptoms and help the doctor make an accurate diagnosis. If a researcher builds up a good rapport with a study participant they are interviewing, the conversation will be better which in turn will assist the richness of information the researcher is able to gather. The ability to quickly connect with others can make all the difference in the emergency services when dealing with others in crisis situations. Think for a minute about the range of professions where rapport is important.

People with learning disabilities have historically been a marginalised group and subjected to situations where their voices are unheard. The UK and many countries have a history where people with learning disabilities were supported within large Victorian institutions, will little or nothing in the way of individualised care. There have been many more recent service scandals involving people with learning disabilities, some of which have hit the media such as the Panorama programme about Winterbourne View.

While abuse may be the extreme, there is also sometimes a more nebulous, perhaps unintentional, style that staff might use that could be regarded as insensitive treatment. These behaviours are less easy to quantify but it could be that staff are very directive, perhaps bossy, or they may be unresponsive to the sometimes subtle communication of a person with a learning disability. These somewhat difficult to quantify staff behaviours are never quite regarded as abuse, but if left unchanged risk continually damaging the relationship that a member of staff has with the person they are supporting.

Having a good rapport with an individual is also potentially essential for achieving specific goals, for example, it is likely to be hard to support an individual to engage in activities if they show no interest in interacting with you. If you need to support someone to develop a person-centred plan, health action plan or learn a new skill, these are more likely to go smoothly if the person is keen to engage with you. Developing a stronger understanding about rapport may help to increase the likelihood of work with the individual being successful.

People we have had a good rapport with in our own lives

When considering how important it is to have a good rapport with a person with a learning disability you support, a great place to start can be thinking about people in our own lives who we have had a good rapport with.

Having a good rapport with a teacher when we are children can make all the difference to having a really successful year at school. If we think about subjects or classes in which we did well during our years at school, the quality of the relationship with the teacher is often cited as a major factor.

To put ourselves in the position of a person with a learning disability it can be most helpful to think about rapport with people that have had some level of power over us or people who are there to support us. Think about people who have been there to support you in the past and the quality of the relationship they have had with you (adapted from Forehand & Long, 1996). Think about the best manager you have had, someone who supported you well. If you are not long out of education you may want to think about a teacher. What were the best characteristics of this person? It may be that words like supportive, good fun, approachable, fair, understanding, warm or generous describe the person, but you are in the best position to produce the list.

Think also about the manager that you have found most challenging to work for or a teacher you found challenging. What list of words describe the characteristics of this person? Perhaps words like negative, critical, unappreciative, unsupportive, bossy or domineering describe them.

Now let's imagine that one of these managers wants you to do a piece of work, an extra piece of work, something harder or more demanding than usual, or something that you will find taxing. Perhaps they want you to stay after work for an hour to help them with something they are doing.

It seems likely that as long as you are able, you will willingly do the extra work for the manager you have a good rapport with. For a manager you struggle with you may take active steps to avoid the demand, partly because you want to minimise the time you spend in their company.

Rapport and behaviour described as challenging

The impact of a poor rapport with support staff is gradually being understood as one factor that can increase the likelihood that an individual will display behaviour described as challenging. So far, research indicates that when staff who do not have a good relationship with the person with a learning disability ask them to do something the request is more likely to be met with behaviour the staff may find challenging (McLaughlin & Carr 2005).

When people with learning disabilities have been asked how they might cope with the situation, if they were supported by staff who they did not have a good relationship with, they have explained that they are more likely to present challenges (Guthrie & Beadle-Brown 2006). The same group of people have identified characteristics of staff who they had a poor rapport with, characteristics included staff who take control or dominate, take over without consulting, are disrespectful or do not show an interest in the person.

Case study: rapport building between Daisy and a member of her support team Ron

Ron

Prior to rapport building Ron described Daisy as being disinterested in talking to him. He said it was difficult to get to know her as she disliked men. Other members of the staff team were all women who said Daisy would never build up a relationship with male staff. This was the message regularly given to Ron.

Daisy

Daisy described Ron as someone who 'kept himself to himself and does not like to chat'. Daisy said she did not like him, and also stated that she generally went home to stay with her aunt when he was on duty.

The home manager and the staff team were fully aware that Daisy would go home when Ron was on duty. If for some reason Daisy had been unable to go home the recording sheets collected about Daisy screaming showed that this behaviour was more likely to happen when Ron was on duty. For these reasons a rapport building intervention was considered important.

It was agreed that rapport building activities would take place a minimum of twice weekly. All activities were identified by both Daisy and Ron as being preferred activities or those that Ron enjoyed supporting Daisy with.

These included:

- going out to the pub
- planning Daisy's weekly activities
- bowling
- cooking a shared meal.

After sharing these activities for about six weeks both Daisy and Ron gave some feedback.

Results

Ron

Ron was shocked at the change in Daisy.
'She keeps talking to me.'
'When she comes in she brings me her bag of shopping to show me what she has brought.'
'She keeps asking when we are doing cooking again.'
'She has not screamed for ages when I have been on duty.'

Daisy

'Ron is alright really.'
'He took me to the pub and we bought a great big meal for £5.'
'I don't always go home now when Ron is on duty.'

How to build rapport with the people you support

Rapport is generally built by spending time with the individual doing enjoyable activities or providing items that the individual particularly likes or enjoys. It works most effectively if you choose an activity that the staff member enjoys too, as in the example of Daisy and Ron, that way the activity can be truly shared. A good guide is to aim for one enjoyable shared activity to take place each time you work with the person you are supporting. Shared activities do not always have to be very time consuming; sharing a joke, a biscuit or a cup of tea take very little time and could be effective in building rapport.

A sensible place to start is to talk to the person and/or others that know them well and draw up a list of activities and items they like. Consider from the list which of those activities you also enjoy and plan to provide one or more of these activities next time you work with the person. Share what you are doing with others in the team as it may be helpful for more than one member of staff in the team to build rapport with the person.

Consider the ways that rapport could become damaged during the course of your working day and try and minimise anything you might do to damage rapport. Acknowledge any attempts the person makes to communicate with you. Try and work out what the person wants if their communication is unclear and make every attempt to provide this. If you need to ask the person to do something do this in a gentle and supportive manner. Include the person in decisions so that they feel in control.

You are likely to know that the rapport building is working well if the person wants to spend time with you, talks to you more frequently, smiles/laughs in your presence and is quicker to engage with you. The person being less likely to present behaviour described as challenging when you are present is another good indicator that you are building rapport effectively.

Rapport building activities may be able to reduce in frequency over time but allowing time to maintain rapport with the person you support needs to be ongoing, so that the positive connection you have built is long lasting and robust.

When rapport is damaged and how to repair it

Rapport can become damaged for a variety of reasons. A member of staff having to break bad news, the use of a physical intervention or being present when an invasive medical treatment took place could all damage rapport. It could quite simply be that a member of staff becomes allocated to another individual, service or classroom and is less available to the individual. Sometimes staff have been hurt or become fearful following behaviour described as challenging and may inadvertently distance themselves from an individual possibly out of fear.

If you have an understanding about why the rapport you have with an individual has become damaged this may be helpful in seeing the situation from the perspective of the person or putting yourself in their shoes. Rapport building activities may need to start again from the beginning or be built up slowly (presented for shorter periods of time) if rapport is damaged.

Summary

- In this chapter we have explored what rapport is and the importance of having a good relationship with the people you support.

- Having a good rapport is likely to be helpful with achieving goals when supporting a person who has a disability.

- There is a link between building a good rapport with people and reduction in behaviour described as challenging. This link is particularly evident if the person is resistant to requests that are made by others.

- We are typically more willing to comply with requests when they are presented by someone who we have a good relationship with.

- Building rapport with the people we support is often fairly straightforward to do. One example is described in the case study of Daisy and Ron.

- When building rapport with a person you support it is also vital to look at the ways rapport may be inadvertently damaged and take steps to minimise these.

References

Forehand R & Long N (1996) *Parenting the Strong-Willed Child: The clinically proven five-week program for parents of two-to six-year-olds.* ERIC.

Guthrie KS & Beadle-Brown J (2006) Defining and measuring rapport: implications for supporting people with complex needs. *Tizard Learning Disability Review* **11** (3) 21-30.

McLaughlin DM and Carr EG (2005) Quality of rapport as a setting event for problem behavior. *Journal of Positive Behavior Interventions* **7** (2) 68–91.

Further reading

Carr E, Levin L, McConnachie G, Carlson J, Kemp D & Smith C (1994) *Communication-based Intervention for Problem Behaviour: A users guide for producing positive change.* Maryland: Paul H. Brookes Publishing Co.

Jensen CC, Lydersen T, Johnson PR, Weiss SR, Marconi MR, Cleave ML & Weber P (2012) Choosing staff members reduces time in mechanical restraint due to self-injurious behaviour and requesting restraint. *Journal of Applied Research in Intellectual Disabilities* **25** (3) 282–287.

Kemp DC and Carr EG (1995) Reduction of severe problem behavior in community employment using a hypothesis-driven multicomponent intervention approach. *Journal of the Association for Persons with Severe Handicaps* **20** (4) 229–247.

Chapter 11: Getting the environment right

By Sandy Toogood

Introduction

This chapter examines the relationship between behaviour and environment. We will review how behaviour changes the environment and vice versa, before considering six types of environments that we all encounter every day. Finally, we will describe how to create an environment that minimises the risk of behaviour that challenges and maximise quality of life.

Behaviour that challenges

Behaviour that challenges is no different from any other behaviour; it has no special qualities other than its effect on people's lives. In most cases behaviour that challenges is learned and continues to occur because of its relationship with the environment.

Environment

The environment includes everything inside and outside of our skin. What we do causes the environment to change in some way, and the way that the environment changes influences what we do. So, if we want to change behaviour, we must think about changing the environment.

Types of relationship

The relationship between behaviour and environment is defined by its effect. The first effect is whether behaviour is more or less likely to be repeated. A behaviour that is more likely to be repeated is a behaviour that has been strengthened. Strengthening occurs when the environment responds either by producing something (like attention) or taking something away (like an activity demand). Both effects are momentary and not a characteristic of an individual.

Why this effect?

Whether the environment strengthens behaviour by producing or removing something depends on the way things are before behaviour occurs. Take chocolate as an example, or your favourite food. Its power to motivate behaviour increases when we have not eaten it for some time. When motivation is sufficient, we are likely to perform behaviour that has successfully produced chocolate in the past. The power of chocolate to motivate behaviour reaches its lowest point after we have eaten it – at that point we are no longer chocolate deprived, we are sated.

Other times the environment responds to behaviour by removing something already present. For example, imagine a colleague asks a junior to do a difficult work task, the junior refuses and the colleague asks someone else. If the junior refuses future requests to do difficult work tasks, it is likely that refusing behaviour was strengthened by removal of the request. Behaviour that challenges may be evoked and maintained by the contingent removal or avoidance of difficult tasks, and very often our behaviour maintains over time according to what we happen to be doing when behaviour that challenges stops.

Before considering the environment further there are three things to bear in mind.

1. Aspects of the environment most commonly associated with behaviour that challenges are a) attention from others, b) accessing things, and c) removing activity or social demands. There is nothing inherently wrong with wanting or needing any of these things; we all seek ways of controlling how we experience the world. The problem is when behaviour that challenges is the only, or most effective, means of doing this. In this sense it is the *means* that are problematic, not the *ends*.

2. Behaviour that challenges becomes the only or most effective means to an end when the environment does not respond equally or preferentially to other behaviour. For example, we might notice every occasion a child throws a cup and overlook every occasion she reaches, smiles, or looks into our eyes. What we need is an environment that responds to all behaviour, making non-challenging, more adaptive alternatives easier, less costly, and more effective than behaviour that challenges.

3. We might think, then, that it is carers/staff/family members who are at fault – that we should know better. However, our behaviour occurs in an environment in which behaviour that challenges also occurs, and that we want to escape or avoid. Without focused effort we will respond in the presence of behaviour that challenges in ways that seem likely to stop it or slow it down in the short term – like providing attention or a cup of tea or sending a person out of class – regardless of the effect these actions may have in the long run. It is not our fault, but there are other more long term options.

Now let's think about types of environment and their effects on behaviour.

Types of environment

The physical environment

The physical environment can influence our behaviour in a number of ways, and it is perhaps easiest for us to see the connection between what we do and how the environment makes repeating the behaviour more or less likely.

You may be able to think of examples of when something you did either produced or removed something in your environment and that made it more likely you would do it again, such as never went back to a café because it was very noisy.

The social environment

The social environment describes our interactions with others, and how those fit with what we want, need, and prefer. Most of us enjoy social contact, and opportunities to spend time with others. As with chocolate, being with others has most value when we haven't done it for a while. There comes a point when the absence of attention from others is enough to motivate behaviour, and behaviour with a history of producing contact will occur. The value of social contact is a very individual thing though. Some of us do not value attention from others in the same way that most of us do. We all engage in behaviour to end a period of interaction, but some us engage in behaviour that keeps people away. The situation in Example 1 shows how staff behave to avoid contact with Laura, which creates conditions under which Laura seeks contact out.

Example 1: The physical environment

Staff avoided spending time with Laura because she could be aggressive and disruptive, and so Laura spent a lot time by herself. When staff came into the same room Laura would often become disruptive. This was because staff attention had become available and Laura was in need of it. Staff thought the disruptive behaviour occurred 'out of the blue' because they could not see that Laura was missing staff attention. Staff used a relaxation procedure to help Laura calm down. This provided Laura with the attention she was missing. When Laura was calm staff would stay away from her to avoid behaviour that challenges, and the cycle began over again. Things improved for Laura and the staff when they began spending more time together at times when behaviour that challenges was not occurring.

The social environment influences our behaviour in more than one way. When it is absent, we behave in ways that produce contact, and when we have had enough, we behave in ways that bring it to an end. A few of us behave in ways that keep others away.

Think about an occasion in your life when you felt alone, neglected, or isolated from a social group, and an occasion when you wanted to avoid contact with others. Recall how this felt, what you did, and how the social environment changed as a result. Is there an occasion in your work or home life when you were not available to others? How did the other person behave, and what impact did their behaviour have on yours?

The tangible environment

The tangible environment is everything in the physical world that exists – anything you can hold, eat and drink. Most of us feel the basic need for food and drink, and, as with the example of chocolate, we feel it most in its absence. The situation in Example 2 shows how a restrictive environment can influence behaviour, how environments can overlap, and how Sheila's behaviour influences the behaviour of staff as much as theirs influences hers.

Example 2: The tangible environment

Sheila spent a lot of time sitting in a chair in a communal area where she lived. About 12 times an hour, sometimes more, Sheila would get up and make a noise – she did not speak words. Staff would say 'Sit down', and she would. Sheila's compliance, and temporary relief from her vocalisations, rewarded the reprimanding behaviour of the staff. Sheila's motivation for getting up every five minutes seemed logically to be related to staff attention, as she received attention each time she performed the behaviour. However, staff had a policy of restricting access to the kitchen. Sheila headed that way every time she stood up because she wanted a cup of tea. Each time staff told Sheila to sit meant she had longer to wait for that precious cup of tea, and so the motivation for tea grew stronger and stronger until she became disruptive. When Sheila showed disruptive behaviour staff gave her a cup of tea to help her calm down. When active support was introduced, the restrictive access policy was relaxed. Sheila has access to the kitchen and made tea with staff support. The cycle of sitting, standing, and vocalising stopped, staff reprimands disappeared, and Sheila gradually spent more of each day engaged in other activities.

These principles apply to the acquisition of food and to activity materials. Again, most of us like to have something interesting to do most of the time, and this usually involves activity materials of some kind (a computer, a book, a TV, a knife and fork, and so on). The value of these items varies in the moment, as does the amount of behaviour we will do to get them, and when we stop doing one thing it is usually to start something else. Changing from a highly valued activity (e.g. reading a book or using an iPad) to something less preferred (washing the dishes or writing an essay) is usually a lot harder than going the other way around.

Think about a time when you needed something to drink, the behaviour you performed and what the environment produced. You may be able to think of a time when your behaviour was blocked in some way – what happened then? Finally, has there been an occasion when your behaviour was an obstacle to someone obtaining a drink, something to eat, or access to a favoured item such as a phone or tablet?

The task demand environment

The task demand environment refers to the pattern, level, and type of activity demand that exists in a person's life relative to their ability to meet those demands, and to their preferences. The level and type of activity demand may correspond perfectly with a person's capacity and capability, so that it is seldom to be avoided. Most of us want to avoid activities that are too difficult, occur too frequently, or that we simply dislike, as with Sarah in Example 3. Sometimes, the environment delays or reduces a demand rather than removing it altogether – so, you might wash the kitchen floor to delay writing an awkward essay or get help on a task you have found difficult.

Example 3: The task demand environment

Sarah worked in sheltered employment and was described by staff as the most productive worker they had. She would pack a consignment twice as quickly as anyone else. Staff thought she enjoyed her work and so they gave her more and more consignments to pack – as soon as she finished one, another arrived. One day she threw everything in the air and overturned her workstation. Later we learned that Sarah did not like packing consignments all that much; she actually worked quickly to get the job done and make time to talk with co-workers. Sarah's workload had increased to a point where the level of demand was intolerable, and she had no opportunity for socialising with co-workers. The environment responded to disruptive behaviour shown by Sarah initially by removing all work demands. Later Sarah's workload was adjusted, and time was made between consignments for her to socialise with co-workers.

Think about a time in your life when one or more of these conditions was true – perhaps you had a difficult assignment to do for a school, college, or university course, or a mountain of washing and ironing to do after a hard day at work. Note the situation, what you did, and what happened to the activity demand – was it removed, reduced, or delayed? Has there been an occasion at home or in work when you increased the level of task demand on others? What did the other person do and what happened to the level of task demand?

The inner-world environment

Most of us has a sense of an inner world that only we can see, but that we can describe to others in words. Our inner world is a type of environment because it influences what we do. For example, when we feel pain, we engage in behaviour to take it away. None of us can access the inner world of another person directly, but we can infer things like mood and pain by observing behaviour. Things affecting the inner world environment include pain, neurochemical imbalances, depression and other mental health difficulties, and some syndromes (causes of intellectual disability).

The inner world environment can interact with each of the 'outer world' environments described above. A good example of inner- and outer world environments is presented in Example 4, which concerns a man called Paul.

Example 4: The inner world environment

Paul had a diagnosis of autism and intellectual disability. He had been prescribed a lot of medication to treat self-injurious behaviour and aggression, but the more he was prescribed the worse the behaviour became. Eventually, it was discovered that the side effects of medication had made Paul feel very unwell. Feeling unwell increased the value of staff attention for comfort, and lowered his tolerance for activity – everything felt like a demand that had to be stopped or avoided, and self-injury was very effective at doing this. Improving conditions for Paul involved changing the inner world as well as the social and demand environments of the outer world. Self-injury was eliminated when medication was withdrawn and focused support provided.

In Paul's case the threshold for tolerating demands and seeking contact was lowered by feeling unwell. Think about a time when you felt ill, perhaps with a headache or a hangover. Then think about the physical environment being too warm or too noisy, or the value of social contact for comfort, and the number of demands you could bear, compared with when you feel well. Was your experience of these things altered by the state of your inner world?

The verbal environment

Uniquely, human beings have the ability to think, read, write, speak, and listen using words. This means we can a) observe and describe relationships between behaviour and environment, and b) form rules about when to and when not to behave in certain ways. The ability to speak and listen spans the inner and outer world environments described previously, in ways that are sometimes helpful and sometimes not. It may be helpful, for example, for us to decide to enrich another person's social environment by ensuring we spend a lot more time with that person. We might make this a formal rule and write it into a plan, or keep it informal and communicate it verbally. Less helpful are the negative stories we sometimes tell ourselves about the type of person we are. Either way, the verbal environment influences behaviour in ways similar to the environments described previously – our behaviour changes the environment, and the change makes it more or less likely our behaviour will be repeated in the future.

Connections

Consequences such as attention, tangibles, and escape overlap one another in ways that can sometimes seem confusing. For example, having a tangible, such as a glass of juice, will sometimes involve the behaviour of someone else getting it for you, which is a form of attention. And, when we escape from an unwanted situation, it is usually to move on to something else that is more preferred, and that may involve contact from others or access to a tangible. However, breaking down these types of relations helps us know what we need to change and how.

Getting the environment right

Understanding behaviour and environment means we can change the relationship between them. This can be especially helpful when we want to improve the quality of our own or another person's life, and when we want to reduce the occurrence and impact of behaviour that challenges.

We can do this in two main ways:

1. By making the environment a better fit to the person's needs there is no need for them to engage in the behaviour that challenges – a sign of a good quality service.
2. We may provide additional focused support for particular individuals based on a functional assessment and with input from specialists.

The final portion of this chapter outlines six steps for environmental adjustments to consider when looking at how to reduce behaviour that challenges.

1. Make the physical environment as comfortable as possible

The first thing is to make the physical environment as comfortable and attractive as possible. Attend to everything that affects the senses, for example, lighting, noise, or odour. In addition, pay particular attention to any physical or sensory impairments a person may have that could alter how they experience the world.

2. Provide plenty of contact, mainly in response to behaviour that does not challenge

Opportunities for social interaction are important to most people but the amount and type will vary from person-to-person and from time-to-time. So, provide as many opportunities for social contact as possible. Make sure everyone has the ability to control when an interaction begins and ends. Include as much variety as possible in the level and type of social contacts available. Make sure there are opportunities for group and individual interactions, and that some interactions are activity-based and some not. Take care to ensure opportunities for social interaction cover the course of a day, a week, a month, and are available in all of the places a person spends time.

Be alert and respond to each person's attempts to initiate contact, and initiate contact with others. In doing so, be careful to respect each person's age and cultural differences, and avoid, for example, speaking to adults as though they were children.

Do not abandon those who seem to avoid social interaction because they seem to be choosing to be alone. Some may not yet have learned how to be with others while others may require additional focused support. Allow people time to be alone, but make sure someone is always available. Look for occasions when a person makes an approach and be available to respond. Create opportunities for contact to occur frequently throughout the day. Make each contact brief and avoid pairing interactions solely with instruction, correction, and activity demands. Instead, pair contact with highly preferred individuals, activities, and foods. Conclude each contact before behaviour that challenges occurs, prompting a non-challenging alternative behaviour that is easy to perform and at least as effective as behaviour that challenges.

3. Minimise restrictions on accessing activity material, food, and drink

Being an adult is partly about being in control and partly about accepting what cannot be controlled. Being a child is partly about moving toward this position. So, impose the least amount of restriction possible for accessing essentials like food, drink, and activity materials in line with age and risk. Manage risk rather than avoid it. Restrictions may be required for some people regarding food, drink, and activity materials for the health and well-being of the person or others. If so, avoid imposing universal restrictions (e.g. no kitchen access), and ensure all personally tailored restrictions are proportionate, specific, time-limited, and frequently reviewed. Wherever possible, provide an alternative to a restricted activity rather than just saying 'No'.

4. Provide support and assistance not demand and control

Most of us are occupied most of the time. Besides going to work, we have hobbies, do chores, and spend time socialising. Being busy is part of a valued lifestyle, provided the level of demand is not excessive. So, provide support and assistance by helping individuals to a) develop and follow personal routines b) timetable activities that occur on a regular basis and c) flexibly fill in the gaps between routine activities so there is always something interesting to do. Finally, be present and provide just the amount of help a person needs at the moment it is needed – do not over help.

Schedules and routines help us be more independent because we know what is expected and what is coming next – we all like to feel we have a degree of control over how we use our time and none of us particularly likes being told what to do and when. More routine means less instruction. In addition, activities become easier when we do them the same way every time, and how we do them is based on our preferences rather than being imposed by others.

Filling the time between scheduled activities creates flexibility and allows us to be spontaneous. It also means we can arrange preferred and non-preferred activities to avoid creating high levels of demand. We can create and manage opportunities for choosing between options by framing the choices that are available. Too much choice can be debilitating, so we might say, for example, 'Would you like to _____ or _____?' or 'We have three things to do, which would you like to do first?' Another way is to use visual supports for 'now', 'next', 'then', and 'later'. These approaches are usually better than open-ended questions like, 'What would you like to do now?'.

With a little bit of planning we can create personal environments that promote autonomy, predictability, and control. The next thing is to deliver exactly the right type of help for exactly the right moment in time. One way of doing this is to view each activity as a series of steps. The amount and type of help can then be adjusted at each step. In this arrangement, a verbal instruction is the least amount of help we can provide. A gesture provides more help than a verbal instruction, and a demonstration more than that, with physical hand-over-hand guidance being the most. When we break activities down like this, and adjust the level and type of help we provide at each step, we increase the chances of success and make participating in activities a more rewarding experience.

5. Observe and manage physical and emotional well-being

Many of the people we support may not yet be able to describe inner-world experiences such as pain or emotional well-being. We must therefore be alert to changes in behaviour and appearance, but also careful to avoid over-interpretation.

6. Have clear methods for expressive and receptive communication

Communication is vital for all of us. One of the most significant things we can do is create a listening environment, one that is sensitive and responsive not just to spoken language, but also to behaviour and appearance.

In regard to behaviour that challenges, however, we must take care not to habituate, to stop noticing, to stop reacting. If we do, behaviour will grow stronger, because the thing that drives it will not go away. We must also take care to listen as attentively to alternate behaviour as we listen to behaviour that challenges. If we want people to do something other than display aggressive or self-injurious behaviour, for example, other behaviour must be at least as effective. This means making sure alternatives to behaviour that challenges are easier to do and at least as likely to be heard.

At the same time, we must make sure our own attempts to communicate are accessible. We should speak clearly, use simple, uncomplicated language, and provide information in manageable amounts.

A number of augmented communication systems exist that use pictures, symbols, and signs. These may help specific individuals, but the most important thing that we can do is to listen.

Conclusion

This chapter examined the relationship between behaviour and environment. We noted how behaviour changes the environment and the environment influences behaviour according to how it is changed. We considered different types of environment that we all encounter and noted how they overlap. Finally, we described how to create environments that minimise the likelihood of behaviour that challenges and maximise quality of life. Every experience we have is added to our learning history. Behaviour that challenges is not inevitable – how we arrange the environment makes a difference.

Further reading

Hastings RP, Allen D, Baker P, Gore NJ, Hughes JC, McGill P & Toogood S (2013) A conceptual framework for understanding why challenging behaviours occur in people with developmental disabilities. *International Journal of Positive Behavioural Support* **3** (2) 5–13.

Mansell J and Beadle-Brown J (2012) *Active Support: Enabling and empowering people with intellectual disabilities.* London: Jessica Kingsley

McGill P & Toogood S (1994) Organising community placements. In E Emerson, P McGill & J Mansell (Eds) *Severe Learning Disabilities and Challenging Behaviours; Designing High Quality Services.* London: Chapman & Hall.

Toogood S (2012) Using contingency diagrams in the functional assessment of challenging behaviour. *International of Positive Behaviour Support* **2** (1) 3–10.

Chapter 12: Keeping people safe – reactive strategies

By John Shephard

Introduction

Knowing what to do in a crisis is an essential element of any support plan: get it wrong and a difficult situation can escalate into a major incident. A tailored reactive strategy maintains everybody's safety and does not aim to punish or correct behaviour that challenges. This chapter identifies a range of non-punishing strategies that are likely to have positive outcomes in the goal of preventing people from coming to harm.

The emergence of positive behaviour support (PBS) has begun to positively impact on the quality of individual plans. Many more people now understand that behaviour does not appear out of nowhere, and they are able to identify antecedents and other predictors of behaviour that challenges. In essence, they understand the need to base support on individual preferences.

Despite improvements, we still sometimes encounter weaknesses in service[1] design in relation to a crucial component of intervention, namely at that stage when the individual has started to move away from their baseline state and are displaying signs of distress, anger, anxiety, or other indicators that something is wrong. These early signs, sometimes quite subtle, can be the precursor to behavioural escalation and potential crisis. It is at this point that the nature and substance of reactive intervention can be crucial and, very frequently, it is the point where things go awry. Very often, this is because, though the service may have a comprehensive range of proactive plans in place for the individual during times of compliance, they have not given sufficient thought and planning to other stages of the behavioural cycle. In these cases strategies for early intervention and reactive plans will either be absent, or lacking in variety and/or person-specific suitability – a 'one size fits all' approach. Typically, such interventions can actually have the opposite of the intended effect, causing the situation to worsen, and creating the risk of people coming to harm. This chapter considers similar common failings in this respect and outlines some more effective interventions.

---

1 Throughout this chapter, *service* and *staff* refer to any setting and its agents where people with challenging needs are supported, including residential services, families at home, teachers at school, and so on.

1. 'It's just one thing after another...' – chains of behaviour

Behaviour that challenges is often predicted by other less impactful behaviours. An incident often builds to a crisis through a chain of behaviours. It can be helpful to conceptualise this journey of escalation as a staircase, with intervention strategies applied according to which step the individual has reached.

Accordingly, it is likely that staff will need a range of agreed responses available to them, beginning by responding at the earliest possible stage. If the individual is on step one (for example, grumpy and disagreeable) it could be that some cajoling, or use of humour, will help them to return to baseline. Behaviours at a higher step may require less transitory responses such as active listening, offering a preferred activity, or some sensitive one-to-one time. If, however, the person is on the top step, displaying their most extreme behaviours, possibly with physical aggression, the intervention here needs to urgently address matters of safety, for example, by:

- **moving others out of the way**
- **removing dangerous items in the environment**
- **containing the area of risk by closing doors**
- **assisting the person to move to a place with calming properties**
- **using a 'hands-on' physical support, for example, holding the person and so on.**

The point here is that what might work at an early stage, may not work later on, so it is essential that a range of strategies are available.

Case example: Lydia

Lydia frequently displayed extremely volatile, aggressive, behaviour in her residential home. For this reason, she was allocated one-to-one staffing, including for the short walk to the day service. One morning she arrived at the day service unaccompanied and showing the early signs of distress. After an interaction with a staff member, the situation escalated into a full-blown incident, placing Lydia and staff at risk. The staff member involved wrote this in his incident report:

'She came in shouting and screaming, and I asked her why she was on her own ... I told her that shouting at me was not acceptable, then told her to calm down but this seemed to make her more aggressive towards me ...'

Give this some thought before reading on.

In this example the question about Lydia being on her own is not neutral: it has a subtext that says 'you are not supposed to be on your own, you're breaking the rules again ...' Given that she was already clearly upset, the staff member might reasonably have guessed that reprimanding her in this way – together with a further reprimand about shouting being 'unacceptable' – would provoke escalation and therefore put himself at risk. A safer option would have been to try to:

- **avoid confrontational approaches**, such as in the above

- **interrupt the chain of behaviour**, by, for example, showing some empathy, perhaps with;

- **active listening**, with a goal of trying to solve the problem that caused her original distress – 'What has upset you?' 'Oh, that happened to me once, and it upset me as well. What I did when that happened was ...'

- **model appropriate responses**, so if the goal is that the person stops shouting, then you would talk quietly to demonstrate what is required, as opposed to giving an order – 'you must stop shouting!' – which can be seen as confrontational.

2. 'The more I told him to stop, the worse he became ...' – behaviour change and behavioural management

In conversations with people working in services we often experience a confusion between 'behaviour management' and 'behaviour change'. These two objectives are very different. Behaviour management focuses on containing and resolving emergency situations, whereas behaviour change is taught in day-to-day support. Behaviour management aims to resolve, behaviour change aims to teach (when the person is not in crisis). Accordingly, when the person has climbed the staircase of escalation, particularly if they are displaying dangerous behaviours, then we need to stop trying to *change* their behaviour, and instead attempt to *manage* it. If there is a comprehensive PBS plan in place to address the longer-term goals of behavioural change, then this liberates the reactive plans in order that they can focus solely on the short-term objective of making high-risk situations safe.

Case example: Joe

Joe is a young man with autism for whom routine is extremely important. For example, each morning he carried out his personal care routine in a specific bathroom in the residential home because this spacious environment suited his particular preferences. After this was completed Joe would move on to his highly preferred activity of spending time on a computer. One morning his support staff member, Dave, started to direct him to the smaller bathroom upstairs. Joe became anxious, since this sudden change of plan was difficult for him to understand, was causing him to use stairs (aversive), and was leading him towards the cramped space of the other bathroom (also aversive). Joe tried to resist, but Dave persisted with his demand, and then Joe broke away and headed for the computer room, where he could see other people using computers. Dave ran ahead of him, closed the computer room door, and blocked Joe's path saying 'No computer Joe!'. At this point Joe's distress turned to anger and he assaulted Dave by punching him in the face.

Give this some thought before reading on.

In this example Dave continues to try to change Joe's behaviour – and achieve compliance – rather than trying to manage the situation and promote safety. When Joe started to show signs of distress, Dave's objective should have been to find a solution that helped to calm him, for example, by:

■ **withdrawing the demand (strategic capitulation)** – postponing (not abandoning) the personal care routine, and

■ **diverting to preferred activity** – 'Okay Joe, let's do some computer, and use the bathroom later'.

In effect, the message of Dave's actions was 'I can see that you're very upset by this change of plan [different bathroom], but if you don't calm down, I'll do this even more upsetting thing to you [no computer time],' and his insistence on trying to change Joe's behaviour during a period of distress resulted in Dave being injured. In fact, after the assault, Joe entered the computer room and logged on, so neither objective, compliance nor safety, were achieved, a common outcome when behavioural change and behavioural management are confused.

3. 'Reward her? Are you joking?!' – do the thing that works

Another effect of liberating reactive strategies from any responsibility other than safety is that it enables staff to intervene in ways that are counterintuitive, in other words to do something that seems at odds with what is recommended at all other times, as in the following example.

Case example: Susan

Susan had a very strong desire to eat chocolate, to an extent that would have been unhealthy if she had free access. Her comprehensive support plan addressed this problem with a wide range of appropriate strategies, allowing controlled access to chocolate. However, Susan also displayed some serious behaviour that challenged, typically involving physical aggression towards others, and requiring rapid, effective intervention. At these times, the offer of a small amount of chocolate typically calmed her immediately. Of course, this seems controversial, and contradictory of the goals of the support plan, and people would cry 'You're rewarding her bad behaviour! You're teaching her to use violence to gain access to chocolate!' and so on. But this is again to confuse behaviour change and behaviour management – the reactive plan here is only responsible for restoring safety, by the most efficient means possible: the problem with chocolate will be addressed through the long-term, proactive plan. In addition, the potentially rewarding effects of chocolate in these instances, and therefore the risk of establishing a relationship between the two (aggression and access to chocolate), are diminished by the fact that Susan has access to it at other, more frequent times, outside of the context of behaviour that challenges.

Imagine the situation where Susan is assaulting her fellow resident Sally: if you prolong the incident by avoiding the most reliable pacifier (chocolate) for fear of rewarding Susan, it is doubtful that Sally would find that to be a very persuasive justification for the beating she received.

The key message here is that, when someone's safety is at risk, it can be appropriate, if not essential, to do something that does not seem to fit with the usual plan, if it has the most likely chance of success.

4.'What are we supposed to do?'

Case example: Marie
During a recent consultation with the author, a staff team described the extreme and highly impactful behaviour of Marie, a young woman in the residential home. A typical scenario involved Marie:

- sitting on the floor
- usually on the first-floor landing
- kicking and lashing out at anyone who came near
- shouting and screaming at the top of her voice
- banging her head on the wall behind her

They were genuinely at a loss to know what to do when Marie displayed this level of distress and aggression, asking, 'What are we supposed to do?'.

Give this some thought before reading on.

Although they struggled to answer this question, they found it a relatively easy matter to answer a different one: 'When faced with someone showing this level of distress, what wouldn't you do?' and quickly suggested a range of ideas:

- **Don't crowd her.**
- **Don't touch her.**
- **Don't shout at her.**
- **Don't give her orders, or instructions.**
- **Don't chastise, criticise or correct her.**
- **Don't repeat utterances she shows no willingness to attend to.**
- **Don't use lots of spoken language.**
- **Don't have more than one person talking to her at the same time.**
- **Don't give contradictory advice.**
- **Don't leave her in an unsafe environment.**
- **Don't make lots of noise.**
- **Don't ignore her and so on.**

Using this self-generated list, they then found it much easier to address the original question – what they should do, as far as possible, are the *opposites* of the strategies on the list, for example:

- **Give her space.**

- **Ask any non-required staff to leave the area.**

- **Turn off sources of extraneous sound – music/TVs etc.**

- **Speak quietly, only one person at any time.**

- **Use neutral, reassuring language, with few words – 'Mum's on her way here'.**

- **Use words that are easy to understand – 'It's okay'.**

- **Avoid giving opportunities for further non-compliance – 'You must calm down!'.**

- **Offer a drink, or another high-preference offering that is known to aid calming.**

- **Make the environment safe by removing hazards, or introducing cushions etc.**

- **Explain what is happening, if necessary – 'I've brought a cushion for your head'.**

It is very likely that, simply by adopting the kind of strategies above, the heat and emotion of the situation will diminish, even if they do not dissipate entirely, and a point will more quickly be reached when a return to baseline is viable. People engaging in high energy behaviours often become tired, and a 'hands-off' approach allows events to take a natural course towards fatigue and calm. It is also noteworthy that the strategies on the above list are actually quite easy to carry out.

5. Restrictive interventions

Despite our best efforts, there may still be times when all non-restrictive interventions have been tried, without success, and the situation remains unsafe. In such circumstances it may be necessary, or even essential, that a restrictive intervention is used, for example, holding someone in situ, using PRN (as needed) medication, preventing them from leaving a building, or escorting them to another area. Such interventions must only be used in accordance with relevant legislation, and a restrictive intervention policy, informed by authoritative guidance, and only by staff who have been effectively trained in how, and in what circumstances, to use them. To justify the use of these interventions, we need to demonstrate that we have considered all alternatives prior to restrictive interventions, that such interventions are clearly described as the final option after less invasive approaches, and that, following their use, people meet to consider how to avoid such situations arising in the future.

Summary of some suggested intervention strategies (with those for the most serious behaviours towards the bottom of the list)

- **Respond to the early signs (precursors) with low-level strategies** e.g. cajoling, humour.

- **Withdraw the demand causing the problem** e.g. 'Okay, you can have your bath later' or

- **Present the demand with an A-B choice** e.g. 'Do you want a bath, or a shower?'.

- **Model appropriate responses** e.g. if they are raising their voice, speak quietly.

- **Active listening** e.g. respond to the message, not necessarily the words they use, so if someone is asking angrily about the time of the next meal, the real message may be that they are hungry – so, perhaps provide a snack.

- **Reduce levels of noise** e.g. music, radios, televisions.

- **Divert to a preferred activity** e.g. 'Hey look! The Simpsons is on TV!'.

- **If you have to say 'no' to a request, suggest a positive alternative** e.g. 'We can't do that now, but what we can do is …'

- **Interrupt the behavioural chain** – any of the above may achieve this, the plan being to avoid doing something that is likely to cause escalation to the next stage of behaviour e.g. by chastising, criticising and so on.

- **Reduce crowds** – including staff numbers, if there are too many.

- **Move others out of the way if high-risk behaviours seem imminent.**

- **Remove dangerous items from the environment** – potential weapons and hazards.

- **Contain the area by closing doors.**

- **Assist the person to move to a place with calming properties** e.g. a quiet area, outdoors in fresh air etc.

- **Use blocking strategies if you are under physical attack.**

- **Use PRN medication.**

- **Use a restrictive intervention.**

Conclusion

When an individual is displaying behaviour that challenges that has the potential to cause high-risk situations, the responsibility of those supporting them is to do what is necessary and legal to keep everyone safe. This will entail:

- Being aware of the early warning signs, and responding to them.

- Being prepared with a range of interventions for different stages of escalation.

- Selecting interventions that are appropriate to the nature, and the level, of the behaviour being displayed, and that have a history of being effective.

- Avoiding those interventions that are likely to present as confrontational, and consequently to cause escalation.

- Remembering that the objective is safety, and not to impose 'the rules', 'teach people how to behave', or to punish inappropriate behaviour.

- Using restrictive interventions if you have to, within the context of appropriate policies and procedures.

Reactive strategies, in the context of a comprehensive support plan, will hopefully be required with decreasing frequency as the benefits of the plan increase over time, and it is essential their use is documented and measured over time in order to demonstrate this. Nonetheless, they are the strategies most likely to determine whether or not incidents of behaviour that challenges result in people being exposed to potential or actual harm, and as such are a crucial component of safe behavioural intervention.

Further examples

Read the following examples and think about how you might approach each situation differently from as described.

Case example: Tony

Tony's staff approached the specialist team with a specific request concerning one aspect of his behaviour. The problem in question was that at meal times, if food had been spilt on the floor, Tony would get down on his hands and knees and gather the food with his hands to eat it. Staff wanted to discourage this behaviour so, whenever it occurred, they would send him out of the room into the corridor until the mealtime was over. This strategy was effective on most occasions, but then one day, when he was on the floor, he absolutely refused to leave, and eventually two members of staff physically dragged him along the floor to the outside corridor. This obviously raised concerns, and they sensibly decided to get some external advice, asking 'How do we safely remove Tony from the room, without risk, when he refuses to leave?'.

Case example: Megan

Megan would often become confused about her plan for the day, and showed distress and anger when her expectations were thwarted. In a typical scenario in the residential home, she overheard another resident, Barry, being told that he was visiting his family that weekend, and so she assumed that she would also being visiting her family. When she excitedly told a member of staff 'I'm seeing my mum and dad tonight!' they replied 'No, Megan, it's Barry's turn to visit family tonight, not your turn'. Megan continued to insist that it was her turn, and the staff member repeatedly told her that she was wrong. Megan became angry and aggressive, and continued to demand that she should see her family. Eventually, after an escalating argument, she was told that if she didn't calm down her next family visit would be cancelled. A full-blown behavioural incident followed.

Further reading

Allen D, McGill P, Hastings RP, Toogood S, Baker P, Gore NJ & Hughes JC (2013) Implementing positive behavioural support: changing social and organisational contexts. BILD, *International Journal of Positive Behavioural Support* **3** (2) 32–41

Beadle P & Murphy J (2013) *Why Are You Shouting at Us? The dos and don'ts of behavioural management*. London: Bloomsbury Publishing.

Social Care, Local Government and Care Partnership Directorate (2014) *Positive and Proactive Care: Reducing the need for restrictive interventions*. Department of Health.

Willis TJ & LaVigna GW (2004) *Emergency Management Guidelines*. Los Angeles: Institute for Applied Behaviour Analysis.

Chapter 13: Learning new ways of behaving

By Ciara Padden & Shelley Brady

Why it is important?

Learning new skills is an important part of life for everyone. We rely on a range of skills and continue learning into old age, whether we are communicating and developing friendships and relationships, taking care of our health, personal hygiene, housekeeping, or taking part in a sport, hobby, or employment.

Learning new skills is just as important for people with intellectual disabilities. However, while the importance of learning new skills is usually recognised in early years and towards adolescence, this can be overlooked in adulthood for many reasons. This can include a mistaken belief that adults with intellectual disabilities cannot learn new skills; uncertainty among staff on how to adapt support to help adults learn new skills; or as a result of behaviours that challenge, which can often consume staff time and resources and result in the development of new skills being overlooked.

Although intellectual disabilities make learning more difficult, all adults with intellectual disabilities, no matter how complex, can learn new skills with the right support. We also know that there are close links between learning new skills and *reduction* in behaviours that challenge. In a positive behaviour support framework, quality of life is viewed as both an intervention and an outcome – if we improve a person's quality of life through supporting them to learn new skills (alongside other appropriate supports, such as establishing capable environments), they will usually engage in fewer behaviours that challenge. Less behaviour that challenges and a better overall quality of life create a win-win situation for adults with intellectual disabilities and those who support them.

But how do we identify the best skills to teach? Before reading the next section, read the case study overleaf and consider the questions that follow.

Case study

Jane is a 29-year-old autistic woman. She lives in a house with four other people in supported living accommodation. Jane travels by bus with support from her sister to visit her family every Sunday. Jane is non-vocal and uses gestures to communicate her needs. Her family describe her as an independent, lively, and sociable person. She also enjoys listening to music and dancing. Jane works in a local charity shop from Tuesday to Saturday where, with some support from staff, she is responsible for washing and ironing the clothes before placing them on the shop floor. The staff in the shop consider her to be an important part of their team and always willing to help in any way she can. Jane reports that she really enjoys working in the shop.

Jane's housemates have recently made a number of complaints to the accommodation manager. They say she is becoming increasingly short-tempered with them. After speaking with the housemates, it transpired that Jane becomes very frustrated with the others when they cannot interpret what she is trying to tell them, frequently throwing items and sometimes physically pushing them out of the way. They reported that when Jane returns from work she paces through the house until the support worker arrives and becomes very agitated if she is not immediately given attention. She insists the staff member prepares her dinner before her housemates. Jane does not engage in any other activities for the evening, continuing to pace and interrupting the activities and conversations of the others living in the house. This is particularly distressing for the housemates on Mondays when Jane is not at work and spends the day at home. Jane also seems to find these days difficult, and spends much of her time pacing the house, humming loudly, and interrupting others. At 9.30pm, staff support Jane in (i) getting clothes ready for the next day, (ii) preparing ingredients so she can prepare her breakfast and lunch the next morning, and (iii) getting ready for bed. Jane is always calm, happy and interactive during these exchanges.

Jane gets up at 7am each morning and prepares her breakfast and lunch as arranged the evening before. She washes and dresses herself in the clothes selected. Staff are available to provide support to Jane during this time. Support staff walk with Jane to the bus stop at 8am where she catches the bus to work. She is pleasant to her housemates during this hour and has shown an interest in helping them with their tasks in the morning, such as loading the dishwasher or making a sandwich if she has time.

- What gaps in Jane's behaviour might be contributing to her engaging in behaviours that are considered challenging?

- What new skills might help Jane so that she doesn't need to engage in behaviours that challenge?

Which skills to teach?

Consider working with an individual and wanting to build on their skills and capacities to engage in their lives in a meaningful way. How is it decided what is most important for the individual to learn?

First, if the person is engaging in behaviour that challenges and the function has been identified using functional assessment, it is usually helpful to teach the person a different way to communicate or otherwise meet this same need. For instance, if a person hits out when faced with a demand, it might be useful for them to learn an immediate way to communicate the need for a break, help, or an end to an activity; or in the long-term to learn the skills needed to successfully complete or even enjoy the activity. This should be individualised, so might include the use of augmentative and alternative communication (AAC) methods such as sign language, picture exchange or the use of a communication application on a tablet or smartphone.

In Jane's case, it is stated that she becomes frustrated when her housemates cannot interpret her communication. Therefore, staff might support her to learn a more effective means of communicating that others can understand. Improving communication would benefit Jane and impact positively on her relationships within her home.

It is also important to consider how to support new skills that might improve a person's overall quality of life. These might be things that help the person become more independent, have more control over their day-to-day lives, or have a greater variety of things to do. The following are some examples:

- Communication. In addition to communication linked to the function of the behaviour that challenges, improving general communication is also likely to be important.

- Choice-making.

- Independence or involvement in day-to-day tasks such as personal hygiene, daily living skills (e.g. meal preparation), and time or money management.

- Independence or involvement in leisure, recreational, vocational or employment activities.

- Social skills and ways to get social interaction.

- Coping, self-management, or communication of health issues (e.g. tolerating visits to health professionals, managing own medication, communicating when in pain).

- Self-management, relaxation, and coping skills, including coping with waiting and delayed access to desired items and activities.

Factors to consider in deciding on skills to teach[1]

When supporting a person to build their skills in a particular area of their life, it is essential that a number of factors are well thought out with careful planning.

1. Preferences and choice

Has the person who will be learning the skill been consulted and involved in deciding the goal? Too often, if the individual does not have an established means of communicating, they get minimal choice in their lives from moment to moment, as well as in long term decisions, which can lead to frustration and in turn behaviours which can challenge others. Facilitating choice is an undervalued method of decreasing behaviour that challenges. It is always possible to provide options to somebody. This can be as simple as ensuring the person can choose a picture of an activity, communicate yes or no through gestures or sign, or even through body language and non-verbal cues, for adults with profound and multiple disabilities. Communication can be learned throughout an individual's life. Being able to get what you need and want is extremely motivating, and when supported systematically through the use of evidence-based practices, all individuals can learn some form of effective communication. It is also important that a person's choices are honoured, as otherwise they will be unlikely to continue expressing choices.

Take the case study of Jane for example. Two scenarios are described where Jane is content and does not engage in behaviour that challenges: (i) when she is working in the charity shop, and (ii) when she is engaged in activities in her home, and it appears that Jane enjoys working in the shop and carrying out specific tasks in her home. On a Monday when she is not working, and during the hours in her home when she is not engaged in activities, Jane struggles. It might be desirable to give Jane a choice of preferred activities to complete during the times where she typically appears to be unsettled and distressed.

2. How will this skill benefit the person?

When deciding with the individual which skills to build, it is vital to consider the impact of these skills on the person at that moment in time and into the future. What might seem trivial to one person could be life changing to the person being supported. Let's consider Jane again. The case study describes times when Jane does not engage in behaviours that challenge. This includes when she is at work or involved in a certain activity, which in turn suggests she finds these activities and being engaged enjoyable. As mentioned above, if Jane could be provided with choice during her 'down time' (those times where she is not engaged, which she appears to find difficult) and learn to communicate the activities she would like to participate in, she might be less likely to engage in the behaviours

---

1 Although beyond the scope of this chapter to discuss in detail, it is worth noting that a number of comprehensive assessment tools exist, which can be valuable for assessing an individual's performance across a range of skill domains. This can be beneficial for identifying a person's strengths and skill domains that could benefit from support, so that appropriate goals can be set. See the end of chapter for further reading suggestions.

that challenge. There are many tasks that Jane could be supported to become more independent with, such as learning to make her own dinner, load the dishwasher, or to do other tasks around the house that she enjoys.

Another area that might improve Jane's quality of life is that of leisure skills (i.e., reinforcing activities Jane can engage in when she is alone or when she is not engaged in a structured activity such as cooking, or working). From the description given of Jane, it would appear that her leisure skills would benefit from some support. These activities would not need to be solitary in nature. Enjoying leisure activities together could be a great way to build relationships and friendships between Jane and her peers. These could be based around shared interests, such as listening to music and dancing. By ensuring Jane has a selection of preferred activities at her disposal throughout the day she is more likely to enjoy herself and interrupt her peers less.

Assessing and teaching skills

Once a skill has been identified as an area of support need for the individual, it is extremely important to consider how the individual will be supported in learning the skill. Bear in mind that the individual has not learned the skill up until this point by watching and imitating in the natural environment (the way many skills are learned), which tells us that he/she needs more support to learn this skill.

Task analysis

When teaching a new skill, a first step is often to break it down into its basic component parts. That is, write down every step of the skill being taught. The process of breaking a skill down into its most basic steps is referred to as task analysis. For instance, in the case of Jane learning to prepare dinner, the first five steps of the process might be:

1. Look at the menu for the day.

2. Take out the ingredients needed for the meal specified on the menu.

3. Wash the vegetables.

4. Peel the vegetables.

5. Chop the vegetables etc.

This process of writing down each step in the process, or chain of steps required for cooking a meal, might end with 'Sit down and enjoy the meal'.

The best way to develop a task analysis is to carry out the task yourself, or watch somebody else do it, and write down each step of the skill until it is completed. A task analysis should be individualised, and for some learners, a more detailed breakdown of the steps might be necessary.

Prompting and prompt fading

Next, it is important to understand the role of prompting in learning new skills. Prompts are additional signals used to increase the likelihood that a person will engage in the correct behaviour at the correct time and experience success. When used, it is also important that we have a plan in place for systematically removing prompts (known as *prompt fading*) as the person becomes increasingly successful with a skill. Otherwise, the person is likely to become *prompt dependent*, meaning that they will become reliant on our support. Effective prompt fading is critical in supporting a person to learn new skills in a successful and efficient manner, as well as reducing frustration for the individual and support staff.

One way of prompt fading would be to use an *Ask – Instruct – Prompt – Show – Guide* approach (see Table 1). Here, the levels of support represent a 'least to most' hierarchy, with 'Ask' representing a lower level of support than 'Show' or 'Guide'. The level support staff provide would be determined in the moment, based on the individual's performance. If the person being supported was not successful with no support or a lower level of support, staff would quickly move up the hierarchy, providing the level of support that leads to success. The aim is to provide the least amount of support necessary to be successful. This does not mean that the person will always need this exact level of support, so the next time the opportunity is presented, staff would again begin with lower levels of support, moving up the hierarchy as needed to ensure success.

It is important to note that any prompt fading hierarchy is intended as a general guide. For instance, if a person has very little understanding of spoken communication, asking or instructing might be ineffective and this might instead be supported with visuals; or if a person has a profound visual impairment, modelling is unlikely to be an effective strategy. This will need to be tailored based on the person's needs. Furthermore, several approaches to prompt fading exist and some people may learn more effectively from using a more errorless approach (see list at the end of the chapter for suggested further reading).

Baseline or present level of performance (PLOP)

Before teaching a new skill, it is first necessary to understand the person's 'present level of performance' (PLOP) for that skill. This provides a baseline so we know what support a person needs and can monitor whether our approaches are effective.

To determine the person's PLOP, the task would be carried out in the way it is normally completed, and staff would record the level of support needed for each step on the task analysis (see Figure 1 for an example). When assessing, it is important not to give support if the person does not need this to complete a step.

Table 1. Description of the *Ask – Instruct – Prompt – Show – Guide* prompt fading hierarchy

Type of support	Description	Example
Ask	Invite the person to complete the task. This is a general verbal prompt and is most helpful when the person knows what to do but does not know when to do it or has difficulty initiating the task.	'It's time to prepare your dinner.'
Instruct	Specific verbal prompts that tell the person exactly what steps to do next or how to do this.	'Take the potato peeler from the drawer.'
Prompt	Using a point, gesture, or other appropriate cue to support the person to perform a correct step.	If the next step is chopping the vegetables and the person is struggling with this, staff might point to the chopping board.
Show	Demonstrating or modelling the step or activity for the individual. Well suited to people with good imitation skills	If the next step is putting the vegetables into a saucepan, this might involve taking some of the vegetables and placing them into the saucepan, so that the person can learn from imitating this model.
Guide	Providing physical guidance to perform a step or activity. This type of support is often necessary for very new tasks, tasks of a very physical nature, or for individuals who have more profound disabilities, particularly if this includes a physical disability.	This might involve hand-over-hand, where you physically guide the person through the step. It could also involve less physical contact, such as gently guiding the person by placing your hand on their wrist or elbow.

Teaching

Once Jane's PLOP has been recorded, staff are aware of what she is currently capable of and the level of support she needs. They are all expecting the same level of skill from Jane, which ensures consistency in the support provided. For example, for steps 4 and 5 in the chain, it has been recorded that Jane can complete these skills independently. Therefore, all staff will know that Jane has the ability to complete these steps in the chain herself. For steps 1 to 3, Jane needs support. So, the main aim is to support Jane in becoming independent in all steps of the chain. Therefore, the level of support, or prompting required, is faded throughout the sessions in order to ensure Jane is working toward her highest level of independence. For Jane, that might be preparing and cooking a meal completely independently, for another that might be sitting and eating a meal independently. It all depends on the individual.

Figure 1: Example data sheet for Jane's meal preparation with PLOP included									
Steps	PLOP		Days						
	Date: 1/2/19	Mon	Tues	Wed	Thurs	Fri	Sat	Sun	
1. Look at the menu for the day.	Ask	A							
2. Take out the ingredients needed for the meal specified on the menu.	Instruct	I							
3. Wash the vegetables.	Prompt (gesture)	I							
4. Peel the vegetables.	Independent	+							
5. Chop the vegetables.	Independent	+							
Legend: + = Independent; A = Ask; I = Instruct; P = Prompt; S = Show; G = Guide									

Factors to consider during teaching

Within teaching sessions, there are various factors that are important to consider.

Direction of teaching

When using a task analysis, teaching can be approached in different directions:

- **Backward chaining.** This would involve initially teaching the last step in the task analysis *only*; then when successful, teaching the last two steps together; and so on throughout the full task analysis. This can be useful if the person is unlikely to attend for a long period of time, since it is initially very brief and the person accesses the end goal immediately. For instance, in Jane's case, after the final step, she would then have a reinforcing outcome of eating her meal (assuming it was a preferred meal).

- **Forward chaining.** This would involve initially teaching the first step in the task analysis *only*; then when successful, teaching the first and second steps together; and so on. Like backwards presentation, this is short but does not have the benefit of meeting the natural end outcome each time. In some cases, however, a task might lend itself to this approach. For instance, if a person was learning how to write their name, it might be confusing to learn this backwards.

■ **Whole task presentation.** This would involve completing all steps of the task analysis every time. Many tasks lend themselves to this approach as they may be difficult to break into individual steps and it can be useful if a person already knows some of the steps in the chain already.

Motivation

We all behave in certain ways because these behaviours have a pay-off or reinforcer. So, when we are supporting people to learn new ways to behave, we need to think about the reinforcer or factors that will motivate the person to use these new behaviours. In the case of Jane's meal preparation, eating dinner would be a natural consequence at the end of this activity.

Sometimes natural consequences are not motivating enough by themselves, and we might need to identify other things the person enjoys and arrange for these to follow the behaviour. For instance, if a person doesn't understand the importance of personal hygiene, the feeling of being clean might not be a very motivating outcome for personal hygiene tasks. In this case, personal hygiene might be scheduled before the person's favourite activity (e.g., gardening).

Even if a person cannot tell us their preferences, we can usually identify their preferences by checking for other non-verbal cues (e.g. choosing pictures, making eye contact, engagement, or smiling vs turning head away, pushing items away, or frowning).

Consistency

It is crucial that all staff are consistent in the way that they are teaching skills to the individual. Otherwise it is likely to lead to frustration and lack of success. Discussions at team meetings, good communication systems, and effective practice leadership can support consistency. The team should agree (and write) a plan explaining how the person is to be supported, when to provide supports, how staff should respond if the person is successful or unsuccessful with a particular step, and so on.

Preparation

Good preparation is key to ensuring a smooth, enjoyable, and successful experience. This might involve checking to ensure required equipment is available and in working order, coordinating with other staff and residents in advance if a specific location or piece of equipment is needed, and having advance conversations with relevant people regarding risk management (rather than risk avoidance). It is also important that teaching is done in an appropriate environment. Trying to do so in an over-stimulating and noisy environment is unlikely to be effective if the person being supported finds noises challenging. What is appropriate will be specific to the individual.

Often staff may find it difficult to find the time to give to individual skill teaching, so preparation and planning is also key here. In some cases, this might be overcome through creative staff allocation. For instance, small group activities where more than one person is interested and in need of learning similar skills can be effective. This also has the added bonus of introducing a social element to the sessions. Where this is not possible, it may be helpful for staff to investigate how they are spending their time. For example, in the case of Jane, it is stated that she insists the staff member prepare her dinner first, before the staff can do any other work. By initially investing time with Jane on learning food preparation and cooking skills, Jane will become more independent and less reliant on the staff member. The staff member can then use that time to carry out other activities and engage with other residents in the house. The other house mates will see Jane engaging in a positive activity and value her role in the house.

Frequent opportunities to practice

It is vital that practice is regular, ideally daily (although this will depend on the skill, since some might be less accessible than others). Regular practice with different staff members and in different environments can also be helpful in ensuring the skill is generalised (i.e. the person is able to use it in lots of different contexts).

Monitoring

It is important to record a person's progress so this can be monitored. In Figure 1, an example data sheet is provided. Each time the person completes the task, staff would note the *highest* level of support the individual required to complete each step (i.e. if staff asked, instructed and used a gestural prompt but only the gestural prompt was successful, this would be noted since this this was the highest level of support given).

The success of the individual is paramount. If they are not learning, then the methods used to teach must be altered. In some cases, it might be a case of reviewing whether enough opportunities are provided, whether all staff are following the same approach consistently, or whether the outcome is sufficiently reinforcing. In other cases, it might mean changing the approach to teaching. There are many other evidence-based approaches to prompt fading (e.g. most-to-least prompting and time delay) and other approaches to teaching skills (e.g. shaping and natural environment teaching) that could also be considered (see further reading list).

It is important to remember that after a skill has been learnt, practice is still important to ensure the person doesn't forget. It can be helpful to maintain a list of learnt skills to ensure these are still being practiced regularly. If a person does forget a skill, this can be retaught.

Summary

■ With the right support and use of evidence-based approaches, all adults with intellectual disabilities can learn new skills.

■ Learning new skills is critical to enhancing quality of life, which is both an intervention and outcome in positive behaviour support.

■ Some new skills might be directly linked to the function of the behaviour that challenges, while others might be aimed at improving overall quality of life.

■ Identifying skills to teach should also involve the individual and their preferences, and should incorporate choice.

■ Skills should be broken down into component steps using a task analysis.

■ A task analysis can be used to identify the person's present level of performance.

■ The task analysis can also be used to teach the skill, using an appropriate prompt fading strategy such as *Ask – Instruct – Prompt – Show – Guide*. The key to this approach is to provide the least amount of support necessary for success.

■ There are many important factors to consider when teaching skills, such as the importance of motivation, consistency, preparation, frequent opportunities to practice.

■ Progress should be monitored and approaches should be adapted if learning is not taking place.

Further reading

Jones E, Perry J, Lowe K, Allen D, Toogood S & Felce D (2017) *Active Support: A handbook for supporting people with learning disabilities to lead full lives* [online]. Available at: https://arcuk.org.uk/publications/files/2017/12/AS-Handbook-updated-2017.pdf – this includes a good description of the Ask-Instruct-Prompt-Show-Guide approach (accessed February 2019).

Matson JL, Hattier MA & Belva B (2012) Treating adaptive living skills of persons with autism using applied behaviour analysis: a review. *Research in Autism Spectrum Disorders* **6** 271–276.

McGreevy P, Fry T & Cornwall C (2012). *Essential for Living: A communication, behaviour and functional skills assessment, curriculum and teaching manual for children and adults with moderate to-severe disabilities*. Orlando, FL: Patrick McGreevy & Associates.

National Professional Development Center on Autism Spectrum Disorder (2019) *Evidence-Based Practices* [online]. Individual modules available for download from https://autismpdc.fpg.unc.edu/evidence-based-practices (accessed February 2019).

Partington JW & Mueller MM (2012). *The Assessment of Functional Living Skills*. California, CA: Behavior Analysts Inc.

Chapter 14: Cognitive approaches to behaviour that challenges

By Stephen C. Oathamshaw

This chapter will discuss the development of cognitive behavioural approaches to the treatment of psychological difficulties in people with learning disabilities, including behaviour that challenges. People whose behaviour challenges services can sometimes access individual and group therapeutic interventions, and case examples will be used to illustrate the use of this approach. Ways of adapting therapy to make it accessible to people with learning disabilities and how to assess an individual's ability to benefit from this approach will also be described. Cognitive and cognitive behavioural approaches to behaviour that challenges are designed to complement other approaches used with individuals and support staff, and can be seen as a key component of the positive behavioural support framework. Empowering individuals to develop ways of managing their own behaviour is a key aspect of this approach.

Cognitive behavioural approaches to anger management have been described since the mid-1980s. Problems with controlling anger are how behaviour that challenges is often described by people who have mild learning disabilities, and anger management continues to be recognised as the area of therapy with the most evidence to support its use. Cognitive behavioural interventions for anger management can be delivered individually or with groups and, although many of the interventions described in the literature have been delivered by psychologists, there is also evidence supporting anger management groups run by support workers and day service staff. There is also now a small evidence base for the effectiveness of other psychological therapies for people who have anger problems such as mindfulness.

Services for people with learning disabilities aim to improve individuals' quality of life in line with the principles of positive behavioural support, government policy documents and clinical guidelines. Behaviours that challenge services include behaviours that make this aim difficult to achieve; including psychological difficulties such as low mood and anxiety, symptoms of psychosis such as auditory (verbal) hallucinations and obsessive or ritualistic behaviours. These behaviours challenge as they may make it difficult for the person to engage in skills teaching or leisure activities and to support to access community resources.

Cognitive behavioural approaches have also been shown to be effective for people with depression and low mood, anxiety difficulties, symptoms of psychosis and obsessive behaviours. People with autism often display behaviours that challenge services and cognitive behavioural approaches have also been shown to be effective for some people with autism. Sexually inappropriate behaviours and sexual offending can also present a significant challenge to services and cognitive behavioural therapy interventions have been shown to be effective with individuals who present these behaviours.

Cognitive behavioural therapy (CBT)

CBT is what is known as a 'talking therapy', which means it is only suitable for people with learning disabilities who are able to use speech to communicate, or have a well-developed alternative communication system such as British Sign Language (BSL). Some CBT interventions, particularly behavioural interventions, can be used with people who have less developed verbal communication, but this therapy approach is not suitable for people with more severe learning disabilities who may have no verbal communication. There are some assessments available for assessing an individual's ability to engage in a CBT approach, but communication assessment conducted by a speech and language therapist should always be considered if it is available.

CBT is based on two basic principles. First, the principle that what we think and feel affects our behaviour and second, that if we change how we think about a situation it can change how we feel and behave. An example may be that if a person thinks they sound stupid when they try and talk to other people in a social situation (thought), they will feel anxious whenever social situations arise (feeling) and will avoid these situations whenever possible (behaviour). The goal of work conducted during therapy and outside therapy during real-life situations would be to develop more positive thoughts such as 'everybody says the wrong thing sometimes' and 'saying the wrong thing doesn't mean people think I'm stupid or a bad person'. Examples of how these changes can be achieved will be described later in this chapter.

Assessing ability to engage in CBT

Since benefiting from CBT requires the cognitive ability to recognise how different situations will make us think, feel and behave, assessments have been developed to assess the cognitive skills that people with learning disabilities need to recognise these links and areas where they may need to develop these skills further. These include assessments for identifying if someone can make an appropriate link between a situation and a simple emotional response (happy or sad), how good someone is at recognising and differentiating behaviours, thoughts and feelings and whether they can make appropriate links between situations, feelings and thoughts, which considers the central component of CBT; how thoughts affect, or mediate, feelings and behaviour.

In addition to considering the cognitive skills necessary to participate in and benefit from CBT, it is necessary to consider other factors that may improve the likelihood of success, or present barriers. Motivation to engage in therapy is key to success, as CBT is an approach where the therapist and participant work together towards an agreed goal, but the participant must be committed to practicing techniques and implementing strategies outside therapy sessions. One factor that can affect motivation is the person's belief in their own ability to achieve change; this is what is known as 'self-efficacy'. Many people with learning disabilities are used to having changes in their lives managed or initiated by carers or staff, and the early stages of CBT are often about supporting people to recognise they can make changes to improve their quality of life themselves, and need to take responsibility for making changes happen.

This is not to suggest that people with learning disabilities are expected to achieve changes designed to improve their psychological well-being and quality of life on their own. Many people with learning disabilities receive support from carers and staff, and the support available to achieve positive behavioural change is often essential to the chances of success and to ensuring that positive change continues after therapy has been completed. Environmental factors such as the person's relationships with staff and people they live with and access to resources can also be crucial to the chances of successful therapy. There are published examples of where lack of sufficient attention to environmental factors has undermined therapy.

Adapting CBT for people with learning disabilities

As CBT is a talking therapy, many of the interventions are verbally based, but can be easily adapted to be more accessible to people with learning disabilities. CBT also essentially includes the use of 'homework' or work done outside therapy to reinforce techniques learnt during therapy sessions, or practice interventions to achieve further learning. An example of this would be a homework task for a person who often got angry when their housemate shouted at the staff. A behavioural recording sheet would be completed during the therapy session detailing how they thought in these situations ('he's trying to wind me up'), felt (angry) and behaved (started shouting at the housemate), and how they may think, feel and behave differently, resulting in a different outcome. The success, or not, of this alternative way of handling his housemate's behaviour would be reviewed in the next session. This way of working is often more effective for people with learning disabilities as it creates opportunities for reinforcing learning outside therapy sessions.

Other ways of adapting therapy include the use of pictures and symbols, simplified visual rating scales rather than numerical, recording forms to be used at home (for example, ABC sheets for detailing anger episodes, although in this context the A is the activating event, B – thoughts, C – feelings and behaviours) with simple language supported by line drawings or symbols.

The anger management programme developed by Taylor and Novaco (2005) contains examples of this sort of recording sheet. The internet can also be an invaluable source of downloadable pictures and symbols that can be used to increase understanding during therapy and the ability to implement agreed interventions at home. Therapy letters are often used in other psychological therapies (for example, cognitive analytic therapy). With people who have learning disabilities, a therapy book developed during sessions and given to the person at the end of therapy can be invaluable. Therapy books can contain strategies, techniques and helpful thoughts learned and practised during therapy, and provide a structured reminder so progress during therapy can be maintained and further developed.

Many of the adaptations described above mean therapy with people who have learning disabilities has a slower pace, takes longer, and incorporates opportunities for repetition and multiple practice of strategies learned outside the therapy sessions.

Staff can also play an important role in increasing the chances of CBT being successful and of positive changes being continued after therapy has been completed. This is one of the key differences between CBT practised in adult mental health settings, where often the therapist and client will meet on a one-to-one basis for an agreed course of therapy and no one else is involved, and the learning disability setting where most clients receive support from staff or carers on a visiting or 24-hour basis. Particularly in group therapy, staff may attend sessions or be available if the person needs a break. For individual therapy, staff are often briefed on what has been covered during a session so that they can support the person with a learning disability to practice strategies (for example, relaxation, or different ways of reacting in an anger-provoking situation) or complete agreed homework such as recording sheets, if required. They may also be asked to support the person to carry out a behavioural experiment appropriately, without giving the person so much support that their belief they cannot do it on their own (for example) is reinforced.

Case study: Sharon

This case example is fictionalised but is based on therapy conducted by the author and his colleagues.

Sharon was a thirty-eight-year-old woman with a mild learning disability. She had suffered from anxiety for most of her life and her mum and dad, with whom she lived until moving into supported living at the age of 30, were also anxious. Sharon was fearful of visiting shopping centres and would only go with a staff member. She had recently started to experience anxiety attacks at home, making her reluctant to participate in cooking, something she had previously enjoyed. An assessment found she was able to make links between situations and how she felt and behaved, and was able to describe some thoughts she had in real-life situations when she experienced anxiety.   →

The therapist worked with Sharon to develop a history, or timeline, of her life and how her anxiety had worsened since she was a young woman.

There were no key events identified, however Sharon had gradually become anxious about more situations and progressively lost confidence to cope with activities she had previously enjoyed as her life became more restricted. Sharon had a belief she was incompetent, having often been told she was stupid at school, and when facing an anxiety-provoking situation had thoughts like: 'I can't do this' and 'everyone's looking at me because they think I'm stupid'.

The assessment information was drawn together into a 'formulation' or explanatory framework that was shared with Sharon to illustrate how her anxiety difficulties were being maintained by her increasing avoidance of anxiety-provoking situations and the best way to address this was to start, with the support of staff, to put herself back into these situations, allowing her anxiety to reduce as she learned she could cope. This strategy of graduated exposure is based on the core behavioural principle of 'habituation', where exposure to a fear (or highly enjoyable stimulus) results in a reduction of arousal (positive or negative) allowing, or in the case of a positive stimulus requiring, repeated and greater exposure. Protective factors identified included Sharon's positive relationships with staff and several relatives who lived nearby.

Intervention included the use of a behavioural hierarchy, rating feared situations ranging from Sharon's least feared – the local shop with a trusted member of staff – to her most feared – the out-of-town supermarket on her own. Staff had a key role, both in supporting Sharon to expose herself to the increasingly feared situations, but also because Sharon had previously sought lots of reassurance from them, meaning she did not learn she could cope with these situations on her own. The therapist also worked with the staff team in helping them to support Sharon during the exposure programme, but without providing excessive reassurance. The therapist and Sharon developed a scale for monitoring her level of anxiety during each shop visit.

Other interventions included canvassing opinions among the staff and others to identify whether other people ever felt nervous about going into busy, unfamiliar environments, or thought people ever looked at them thinking they looked stupid. The results from this 'survey' were shared with Sharon, demonstrating others also sometimes experienced these thoughts. This information surprised Sharon as she thought other people didn't think like that and it was used to question her negative beliefs, which underpinned her anxious feelings. Other behavioural approaches included the introduction of a relaxation programme at home, again supported by staff, and a list of activities Sharon could try when feeling anxious such as listening to her favourite music, or having a bath with aromatic bath oils.

The therapist worked with Sharon until she had made significant progress accessing feared environments. As anticipated, her anxiety reduced and her negative thoughts in these situations were increasingly replaced with thoughts like 'I can do this'. A therapy book was produced with Sharon and a final meeting with her and the staff team was used to ensure everyone understood what more was needed to help Sharon continue to progress.

A follow-up session with Sharon three months later found she had continued to visit larger shops with minimal staff support and the final feared environment (the out-of-town supermarket) was next on the list.

This chapter has discussed the small but growing evidence base that shows that adapted CBT can be effective with people who have learning disabilities and whose behaviour challenges services. Ways of assessing someone's ability to access CBT were detailed and a range of methods for adapting therapy to make it accessible for people who have learning disabilities were illustrated.

As with other approaches to people whose behaviour challenges services, a key aim of adapted CBT is to improve a person's quality of life, in this case by empowering people to learn ways of managing their psychological difficulties more effectively, thus allowing them to access environments and activities that enrich their lives. The examples discussed and the case study demonstrates that the success of individual CBT can be very reliant on support from staff and support workers can play a crucial role with this approach, as with other interventions, to support people whose behaviour is challenging more effectively.

Conclusion

- There is now a small evidence base that a therapy with considerable evidence of effectiveness for people with mental health problems can also be effective with people who have learning disabilities and whose behaviour challenges services.

- To be effective with the people we support, CBT has to be adapted to take into account people's cognitive difficulties. This chapter has discussed such adaptations.

- Support workers can be crucially important in helping with CBT interventions and supporting individuals to benefit from therapy.

- With these adaptations and support, people with learning disabilities can be empowered to manage their psychological difficulties more effectively and improve their quality of life.

Reference

Taylor JL and Novaco RW (2005) Anger Treatment for People with Developmental Disabilities. Chichester: Wiley-Blackwell Ltd.

Further reading

Oathamshaw SC (2007) Delivering cognitive behavioural therapy in community services for people with learning disabilities: difficulties, dilemmas, confounds. *Advances in Mental Health and Learning Disabilities* 1 (2) 22–25.

Singh NN, Lancioni GE, Karazsia BT, Winton AJW, Myers RE, Singh ANA, Singh AHA & Singh J (2013) Mindfulness-based treatment of aggression in individuals with mild intellectual disabilities: a waiting list control study. *Mindfulness* 4 158-167.

Taylor JL, Lindsay WR, Hastings RP & Hatton C (2013) Psychological Therapies for Adults with Intellectual Disabilities. Chichester: Wiley-Blackwell Ltd.

Willner P, Rose J, Jahoda A, Stenfert Kroese B, Felce D, MacMahon P, Stimpson A, Rose N, Gillespie D, Shead J, Lammie C, Woodgate C, Townson JK, Nuttall J, Cohen D and Hood K (2013) A cluster randomised controlled trial of a manualised cognitive–behavioural anger management intervention delivered by supervised lay therapists to people with intellectual disabilities. Health Technology Assessment 17 (21) 1-173.

Chapter 15: The use of medication for the management of behaviours that challenge in people with intellectual disabilities

By Shoumitro Deb

Summary

The use of medication for the management of behaviours that challenge in people with intellectual disabilities may have to be considered under certain circumstances, but they should only be used if the behaviour poses a major risk and other ways of managing behaviours have been unsuccessful. Medication should only be used after a comprehensive, person-centred assessment of the causes and effects of behaviours and a formulation that describes the rationale for its use. The outcome and adverse effects should be monitored at a regular interval and withdrawal of medication and use of non-medication-based management should be considered at regular intervals.

Introduction

There are many reasons why people with intellectual disabilities show behaviours that challenge. These include biological factors such as genetic disorders, psychiatric disorders, psychological factors such as cognitive impairment, and social factors such as the wrong environment, sensory sensitivities and lack of meaningful day activities. Given the multi-factorial nature of these behaviours it is imperative that an inter-professional approach is taken to address them and non-medication-based behavioural and psychological approaches should be tried first. However, sometimes medication is used either alone or in combination with non-medication-based interventions. Medications that are used to address these behaviours are collectively known as psychotropic drugs and were originally used for the treatment of various psychiatric disorders. Psychotropic medications used for behaviours that challenge in people with intellectual disabilities include antipsychotics (neuroleptics), mood stabilisers, antidepressants, anti-anxiety, psychostimulants, opioid antagonists, beta blockers and so on.

Antipsychotics

Antipsychotic medications are primarily used to treat psychoses such as schizophrenia and also mania and hypomania. Older antipsychotics include haloperidol and chlorpromazine. However these medications may have serious adverse effects such as extrapyramidal symptoms that include acute dystonia (sudden abnormal posturing of the body), Parkinsonian symptoms such as stiffness, slowed movement, tremors, akathisia (internal and external agitation), and tardive dyskinesia (long-term adverse effect with abnormal face and body movements characterised by chewing and sucking movements, grimacing, and slow turning movement of the head and limbs), as well as dry mouth, blurred vision and constipation.

Antipsychotic treatment can worsen seizures if the person has epilepsy or induce epileptic seizures in people who did not have epilepsy before. Other adverse effects are cardiac (abnormal heart rhythm such as prolonged QT interval) and sexual dysfunction (impotence, lack of libido etc.), and metabolic such as raised prolactin level (the hormone that tells the body to produce breastmilk). One serious adverse effect is neuroleptic malignant syndrome (NMS). This is a rare but potentially fatal condition characterised by high body temperature, muscle rigidity, fluctuating blood pressure and levels of consciousness. This can be treated but requires hospitalisation.

Newer antipsychotics are risperidone, olanzapine, quetiapine, clozapine, aripiprazole, paliperidone, amisulpride, ziprasidone, zotepine and so on. Possible adverse effects are extrapyramidal symptoms, metabolic syndrome such as glucose intolerance (leading to diabetes mellitus), and weight gain. Other adverse effects are drowsiness, blood abnormalities such as agranulocytosis (particularly associated with clozapine), and sexual dysfunction. Other metabolic abnormalities include raised cholesterol and prolactin. Therefore, regular blood tests and possibly an ECG are necessary to check for these adverse effects. Newer antipsychotics are now used more often than the older ones.

There is moderately strong evidence to show that risperidone could be effective for behaviours that challenge particularly among children with intellectual disabilities and with or without autism spectrum disorder (ASD). However, the evidence for adults is uncertain. The main concern is about excessive daytime sleepiness and weight gain. A drug company has conducted a couple of studies that showed aripiprazole improved behaviour among children with ASD. In the US (but not in the UK), both risperidone in low dose and aripiprazole are approved for treatment of agitation in children with ASD.

Mood stabilisers

Mood stabilisers are primarily used for the treatment of mania and hypomania (bipolar affective disorder). Mood stabilisers include lithium and some antiepileptic medications such as sodium valproate and carbamazepine. Regular blood tests are necessary to monitor lithium levels in the blood and its adverse effects include tremor, swelling of feet, excess thirst and frequent passing of urine, kidney failure and thyroid dysfunction. Lithium toxicity can cause confusion and lead to death. Therefore, it is difficult to use lithium for those who have limited capacity to give informed consent and for whom regular blood tests are difficult to carry out.

Carbamazepine (tegretol) is used for the treatment of simple and complex partial seizures and tonic-clonic seizures secondary to focal discharge. It should be started at a low dose and gradually increased. Possible adverse effects are drowsiness, double vision, ataxia (problems with balance), hyponatraemia (low blood sodium levels) and skin rash (may lead to Stevens-Johnson syndrome, which is a serious condition). Sodium valproate (epilim) is another antiepileptic medication which again, should be started at a low dose and then gradually increased over time to minimise adverse effects. Possible adverse effects are drowsiness, weight gain, hair loss, skin rash, ataxia and impaired liver function in some cases. Sodium valproate cannot be prescribed for women in child bearing age because of its potential adverse effect on the foetus. At present, there is no convincing randomised controlled trial-based evidence to support any of the mood stabilisers use for behaviour management in people with intellectual disabilities.

Antidepressants

Antidepressants are primarily used for the treatment of depression. For the treatment of depression, it is necessary to take this medication for a couple of weeks before any effects could be seen, and the treatment may need to be continued for at least six months. Antidepressants may also be used to treat generalised anxiety disorder, social anxiety, obsessive compulsive disorder, and post-traumatic stress disorder. People with intellectual disabilities could suffer from a depressive disorder and may express this outwardly by exhibiting behaviours that challenge. Old generation antidepressants are those such as amitriptyline, clomipramine, imipramine. Possible adverse effects are dry mouth, constipation, urinary retention, blurred vision, low blood pressure, heart failure, fatality associated with overdose. These medications are now rarely used.

New generation antidepressants are selective serotonin reuptake inhibitors (SSRIs) such as fluoxetine, fluvoxamine, sertraline, citalopram, escitalopram, paroxetine, and selective nor-adrenaline reuptake inhibitors (SNRIs) such as venlafaxine and duloxetine. Other antidepressants are mirtazapine, flupentixol, reboxetine and tryptophan. Possible adverse effects of these medications are agitation, sleep problem, sexual dysfunction, the problem with withdrawal and serotonin syndrome (associated with SSRIs). Currently, there is no strong evidence in support of antidepressants' efficacy for behaviours that challenge. Case studies showed improvement in behaviour in some, the rest either did not improve or deteriorated. Most pronounced effect on behaviour is shown when the person has anxiety/depressive or obsessional symptoms. However, most studies reported adverse effects which sometimes made behaviour worse.

Other medications

Although there is little evidence to support the use of other medications for behaviour that challenges such as anti-anxiety drugs (benzodiazepines such as diazepam and lorazepam; and buspirone), opioid antagonists (naloxone, naltrexone), psychostimulants (used for children with attention deficit hyperactivity disorder; ADHD) such as dexamphetamine, atomoxetine, methylphenidate, beta blockers (propranolol, atenolol) etc, they are still used.

Withdrawal studies

Studies have shown that on average in 50-60% of cases antipsychotics could be either withdrawn completely or the dosage reduced after long-term use. Encouragingly, one study found 66% (55/83) of individuals remained antipsychotic-free almost 10 years after withdrawal. However, a subsequent study showed that unfortunately, it becomes difficult to withdraw antipsychotics altogether in a very high proportion of those who had a relapse of behaviour after one or two attempts of withdrawal. However, the withdrawal is only possible if an active programme of antipsychotic withdrawal is implemented. Carers' attitude and perceptions seem to influence the success of withdrawal. Greater restriction and lesser scope of adaptation within the living environment, poor staff training and organisational policies, and both clinicians' and care staffs' lack of confidence in dealing with transient behaviour change upon withdrawal of medication, are some of the important factors affecting the success of withdrawal. Proper training and support for care staff is thus of paramount importance to make the withdrawal successful.

Studies have shown either no change in behaviour or improvement after withdrawal of antipsychotics in most cases, but others showed worsening of behaviour in some. Several studies showed that withdrawal of antipsychotics (particularly the old generation ones like chlorpromazine, haloperidol etc.) may precipitate extrapyramidal symptoms, particularly dyskinesia, which may lead to deterioration in behaviour in some. However, most studies show that these symptoms improve after a few weeks and months. This is an important learning point for clinicians who are considering withdrawal of antipsychotics, so that instead of re-instating antipsychotics straight away because of the resurgence/worsening of behaviour after withdrawal of antipsychotics, they should wait (if necessary with the help of an a PRN (as needed) prescription) until the behaviour improves (see Case studies 1 and 2).

Case study 1: Unsuccessful withdrawal of antipsychotic medication

A 68 year-old-man with mild intellectual disabilities who developed dementia was treated with risperidone for many years because of a past history of aggressive behaviour. After three months of gradual withdrawal of risperidone, the man became physically aggressive on one occasion in an evening club. The care staff panicked, and local police were called out at night, which led to reinstating of risperidone by an emergency doctor.

Case study 2: Successful withdrawal of antipsychotic medication

A 26 year-old man with severe intellectual disabilities who had no speech became disturbed when his risperidone, which he received for many years, was gradually withdrawn. The care staff became very anxious and there was pressure on the clinician through the GP to reinstate risperidone. However, the clinician explained to the care staff that sometimes after years of use, drug withdrawal may worsen behaviour, sometimes caused by withdrawal dyskinesia. The man was treated with PRN (as required) medication over the next three months and his behaviour gradually settled without requiring any regular medication.

Clinical guideline

Here are some examples of when clinicians may consider medication for the management of behaviour:

1. The behaviour causes a major risk, distress and/or harm to the person themselves or others, to property or any other potential severe consequences of the behaviour.

2. Failure of other non-medicinal interventions.

3. Success of medicinal intervention before.

4. Underlying mental disorders such as psychosis, depression, anxiety, ASD, ADHD etc.

5. As an adjunct to other measures.

Sometimes the person with intellectual disabilities or their carer may choose to have medication as a treatment option. In those cases, a full discussion is necessary with the person with intellectual disabilities and other relevant professionals.

Any option including the use of medication should depend on a comprehensive, holistic, person-centred assessment of the cause and effect of the behaviour which should lead to a formulation and rationale for use of the proposed treatment, including the use of medication. It is important to include the person with intellectual disabilities where possible and/or their carer from the outset in the discussion/decision about using medication. Where possible it is a good practice to involve members of a multidisciplinary team such as the community learning disability team. Once prescribed it is important to monitor the outcome of the treatment and any adverse effects, where possible using standardised outcome measures. It is essential to assess the person's capacity to give informed consent to the treatment at the outset, and if they do not have capacity, medication should only be used if it is deemed necessary in the person's best interests. However, it is important to keep in mind that people with intellectual disabilities may need some help with their communication so information about treatment should be presented in an accessible format. Medication should only be used while it is legally permitted. While assessing the outcome of the treatment, it is important also to assess the person's and the carer's quality of life.

Assessment

Assessment and formulation should include identification of the behaviours that are challenging, their causes and consequences. The likes and dislikes of the person and their strengths and weaknesses should be explored using a person-centred assessment approach. Medical factors such as an underlying medical problem, pain in the body, physical discomfort/disabilities and psychiatric disorders should be explored as a possible cause of the behaviour and treated accordingly (see Case studies 3 and 4). Psychological factors such as the person's emotional make up and cognitive impairment should be considered when formulating treatment options. Social and environmental factors such as an overcrowded environment, lack of meaningful day and leisure activities should be addressed before considering any use of medication. These assessments may lead to non-medication-based interventions devised by professionals from a multi-disciplinary team (see Case studies 5 and 6). Predisposing (such as genetic disorders), precipitating (such as stressful life events) and perpetuating (lack of appropriate care support) risk factors should be assessed and considered, and a full assessment of risk to the person and others should be implemented. Before considering medication, all other options should be considered. The rationale for the use of medication, and desired and undesired effects of the interventions should be considered at the outset and monitored on a regular basis. The treatment plan should be part of an overall person-centred plan. At regular intervals, the possibility of withdrawing medication and use of alternative methods of management should be considered.

Case study 3: The role of medical problem in causing problem behaviour

A 65-year-old woman with severe intellectual disabilities suffered from a stroke that led to paralysis of the right side of her body. She started screaming and shouting regularly and the care staff asked for psychotropic medication to manage her behaviour. However, close examination revealed that the lady developed spasticity in her right hand and she was constantly getting frustrated by not being able to stretch the fingers of her right hand, which led to screaming. Instead of psychotropic medication, baclofen was prescribed as a muscle relaxant and the woman's behaviour improved.

Case study 4: A medical symptom leading to problem behaviour

A 75 year-old man with moderate intellectual disabilities and limited communication skills developed symptoms of dementia. He started screaming and banging his head. His sister who is his primary carer asked for psychotropic medication, but the clinician prescribed paracetamol assuming that the behaviour may have been precipitated by headaches. This has produced a good result and the gentleman stopped screaming and head banging.

Case study 5: The role of non-medication-based intervention

Care staff in a community group home wanted psychotropic medication for a 27-year-old man with severe intellectual disabilities and no speech because of his behaviour. Further assessment revealed that the person becomes agitated when he is not allowed to go out for a car ride which he enjoys. A speech and language therapy assessment revealed that care staff were telling the person, 'You can't go out in a car' and the moment the person heard the word 'car', he thought he was going out, and became very frustrated and disturbed as he was not allowed to go out. The speech therapist devised a picture board with 'a picture of a car crossed out', which the care staff showed when the person was not allowed to go out and kept him engaged with alternative activities within the house that he enjoys. This strategy worked, and his behaviour improved without the need for any psychotropic medication.

Case study 6: The benefit of multi-disciplinary involvement

Care staff asked for psychotropic medication to control the behaviour of a 36-year-old woman with moderate intellectual disabilities who has no speech. Further assessment by a speech therapist revealed that the care staff usually ask the woman what she wants for her dinner and give her two or three choices. She always opts for the last option but when the food is served, she refuses to eat it and becomes disturbed. A speech therapist suggested that instead of giving her choice verbally, the care staff should show pictures of different meals and also involve her in the preparation of her meals. This strategy worked, and her behaviour improved without any psychotropic medication.

Recommendations for the person administering the medication

People administering the medication should have basic knowledge of the purpose of the treatment, different types of medications used, common and serious adverse effects of these medications and the action necessary to deal with them, and of any contraindication for not using the medication. People administering the medication should check that it is administered at the correct time of the day (also in relation to meal times). The sequence for giving several medication should always be appropriate and the right dose must always be administered. If in doubt, people should always check the instruction given by the prescriber or check with another staff member or the British National Formulary (BNF).

Communication with the prescriber is very important, particularly if any changes to dosage have been made. All those involved in administering medication should be up-to-date with any recent changes in the dose. Recent loss or gain in weight, possible allergies and the correct measurement for liquid formula should always be considered. People should be sure about the route of administration of medication, and of any recent changes in the instruction. People should have the right training before administering any medication (for example, administration of rectal diazepam or buccal midazolam). People should ensure that they have the right level of competence to administer medication. They should always ensure that the correct and safe instruments are used. The person should be monitored to ensure that they do not spit the medication out or develop any adverse effects. All records should be kept in line with policy, regulations and best practice. The records should be legible and written in an understandable way. The records should be kept confidential and up-to-date, and monitored regularly. Accessible versions of information leaflets on psychotropic medications with accompanying audio versions are available for free download from www.ld-medication.bham.ac.uk.

Further reading

Deb S (2016) Psychopharmacology. In: NN Singh (Ed.) *Handbook of Evidence-Based Practices in Intellectual and Developmental Disabilities, Evidence-Based Practices in Behavioral Health* (pp347–381). Switzerland: Springer International Publishing.

Deb S, Kwok H, Bertelli M, Salvador-Carulla L, Bradley E, Torr J & Barnhill J (2009) International guide to prescribing psychotropic medication for the management of problem behaviours in adults with intellectual disabilities. *World Psychiatry* **8** (3) 181–186.

Unwin GL & Deb S (2010) The use of medication to manage problem behaviours in adults with a learning disability: a national guideline. *Advances in Mental Health in Intellectual Disabilities* **4** (3) 4–11.

Part 4:
Lessons Learned

One of the important elements of good support is the need to look after each other and ourselves. This section therefore is reflective in nature. If we don't think about what we've learned, lessons can easily be forgotten. This section considers the real experiences arising from supporting people whose behaviour challenges us, and the implications for practice. We cannot deal with behaviour that challenges alone. No single profession or individual 'owns' expertise about behaviour that challenges and we have few options apart from remembering the need to work in partnership with those who are as committed as we are to the well-being of the person using services.

Chapter 16: We are all in this together: supported staff

By Peter Baker & Nick Gore

Does behaviour that challenges cause staff stress?

At first glance it would appear to be an obvious statement that working with people with intellectual disabilities who present behaviour that challenges is stressful, and has a negative impact on the psychological well-being of staff. Indeed, there is some research that suggests staff who provide direct care to people with behaviour that challenges are particularly prone to experiencing stress and burnout. However, and perhaps surprisingly, the link between behaviour that challenges and negative emotional states for staff is not always straightforward, and in some studies not evidenced at all. What appears to be the case is that whilst experiencing and managing behaviour that challenges can be difficult for staff, there are other factors that influence how the member of staff actually feels and responds to these feelings.

Research has identified the complexity of what determines well-being of staff in these situations and has concluded that it is often the characteristics of the organisation that provides the support to the person that are more important determinants than the behaviour itself (Hatton *et al*, 1999). These include how the care is organised, the clarity of the roles that staff have, and the extent to which staff are supported by the organisation. Individual factors specific to each member of staff have also been shown to be influential. The beliefs and attributions a staff member has in relation to a person with a learning disability, and why they engage in the behaviour that challenges, are all important in determining how they feel if and when exposed to an incident. For example, a staff member would be more likely to experience a negative emotional reaction if they think the person has control over how they are behaving, that 'they are doing it on purpose', or 'doing it to wind me up' etc. Similarly, the extent to which a staff member feels able and equipped to cope (both with the behaviour they are exposed to and their own emotional states) will have an influence, as will any pre-existing mental health problems the staff member has that may not be directly related to their work.

Thus, an incident that occurs in a well-organised service, with good positive behavioural support, which clearly defines what staff roles are and supports staff in their work with good training and supervision, would be less likely to have a negative impact on the emotional well-being of staff than the same sort of incident occurring in a poorly organised service. Furthermore, even within a service or organisation, the same type of incident would be experienced differently according to the individual staff member's beliefs, attributions, coping mechanisms and resources, and pre-existing mental health.

Case example

Paula is a direct support worker in a service where occasional incidents of behaviour that challenges occur. She has had a few days of mandatory training and believes the main focus of her job is to provide basic care for the people who live in the service. She also has concerns and worries in her own family life, specifically about her teenage daughter who is failing at school. She experienced an incident at work and took it really badly. John, a person with a learning disability who lives in the house where Paula works, lashed out at her whilst she was providing personal care. Paula felt both frightened and let down by John – 'That's the thanks he gives me for trying to clean him up, and on top of all the problems I have right now'.

Eventually Paula was taken aside by the house manager for what he/she called 'a debrief'. During this time Paula was asked to tell the manager what happened and explain what went wrong so that a similar incident would not occur again in the future. Paula did not experience this as positive and felt resentful towards the manager. She felt she was being blamed for the incident. She felt the manager should have been more sensitive given that she was experiencing problems in her home life, even though she had not told the manager about the problems with her daughter. Her attitudes hardened after this and she became frightened of John and did all she could to try to get out of working with him in case she did something wrong. When she could not avoid it, she did all she could to get the personal care over and done with as quickly as possible.

What were the factors that influenced Paula's negative emotional experience of the incident?

How well do you think the manager handled the situation? How might it have been handled better?

Why support the emotional well-being of staff?

Employers have a legal and moral responsibility to maintain the well-being of their workforce, with the obvious additional payoff of reduction in sickness rates and staff turnover. But there is also a link between any emotional impact of the behaviour that challenges and the staff member's ability to provide appropriate positive behavioural support (PBS) (see Chapter 4). The implications are that staff who are feeling stressed or burnt out could well behave in ways that either trigger an incident or makes behaviour that challenges more likely to occur in the future.

Consider a situation where a member of staff has experienced a person they support engaging in behaviour that challenges, such as self-injury or aggression, directed at them. As a result, and in combination with other organisational and personal factors, they may experience a range of negative emotional states such as low mood, anxiety, fear, etc. Part of the consequence of this might then be an impact on the staff member's ability to respond in a helpful manner to the person when they next need support. For example, low mood might make interacting with the person aversive or at least less pleasurable, and fear might make the interaction fraught. As a result, the staff member might be less inclined to spend time with the person because they find the interaction aversive, or for fear of triggering an episode and perhaps getting hurt themselves. None of this is inevitable, but could well be more likely to occur (and providing good support in such a context would undoubtedly be very challenging).

In a similar way, the staff member's responses at the time of actual incidents of behaviour that challenges might also be affected in unhelpful ways. For example, if the staff member is experiencing low mood or anxiety, it is likely to make the episode even more frightening or distressing. As a result, the staff member might well seek to terminate the episode, or any interaction, as quickly as possible, whatever the longer-term consequences might be. Consider Paula, her emotional state undoubtedly got in the way of her providing the care John needed.

So, we can see that negative emotional states of staff can serve as a condition where behaviour that challenges is more likely, as we know that low levels of engagement, and poor quality of social interactions, are all contexts in which such behaviour is likely to occur. Furthermore, the staff member being focused solely on wanting the incident to stop as quickly as possible could create a condition where behaviour that challenges is reinforced and more likely to occur over again. None of this is the 'fault' of the staff member. It is just what people are likely to end up doing given certain conditions and experiences.

On the positive side, staff who have reasonable levels of well-being, and are well supported during periods of emotional difficulty, are more likely to have the necessary resources to be able to make greater efforts to provide good support and follow PBS plans. Thus, we can see how vital it is for services to actively attend to the psychological well-being of their staff. Services are legally obliged to ensure the well-being of their staff and, furthermore this directly impacts on the quality of service provision and behaviour and well-being of people who use those services.

A multi-tiered model of staff support

We are all in this together, and just as we strive to create supportive environments for people with intellectual disabilities who have previously engaged in behaviour that challenges in order to get their needs met, we must also have psychologically healthy and resilient staff in order to achieve this.

In the PBS framework we identify strategies for the prevention of the behaviour that challenges (primary prevention); strategies to prevent escalation, brought in to play when the early warning signs are apparent (secondary prevention); and then reactive strategies to cope with behavioural crises when these occur.

The PBS model is underpinned by an endeavour to understand *why* people engage in behaviour that challenges, and to provide supportive, person-centred environments and skills teaching that increase quality of life, rather than simply manage the behaviour by aversive punishment. Yet, all too often these standards do not apply to the way we treat staff. We are not clear as to their roles, we give them little training, use ineffective teaching methods and then punish them when things go wrong, often ignoring the extent to which they have been emotionally impacted by the incident.

Consider Paula, was she prepared properly for the role of direct support for John, did she have adequate training? How helpful to Paula was the 'debrief' offered by the manager? Although one of the intended purposes of this may well have been to offer emotional support, this was lost on Paula. She only experienced being held to account and blamed for the incident. Given that staff are one of the most important resources for the vast majority of people with intellectual disabilities who rely on services to meet their needs, it is argued here that we need a systematic approach to organising staff support. This should primarily focus on establishing and maintaining staff well-being, but should also include clear procedures for supporting staff when they experience incidents that could potentially impact on their well-being. Such a model is presented in Figure 1.

Universal supports/primary prevention

Recruitment and training

It is vital that staff know what their role entails; they need to know that they are there to promote active engagement, independence and inclusion, and generally to enable the person to achieve a good quality of life based on the aforementioned principles. This person-centred approach is at serious odds to a role which focusses on just the provision of basic care, a role that would be akin to being a 'childminder' or 'hotel worker' (see Chapter 9). Taking on this role will not happen by accident, and the nature of the job needs to be explicit when recruiting staff, and staff need to be trained. This training should be based on, and thus reinforce, person-centred values, as well as providing competencies around how they can be achieved. This training will of course involve some traditional lecture/classroom element, but this alone is unlikely to be sufficient. More importantly, the training should be based on the principles of coaching, where the staff member is taught to do their job in the workplace setting. This would involve observing other competent staff and engaging in coached reflective practice.

Figure 1: Multi-tiered organisation-wide positive staff support

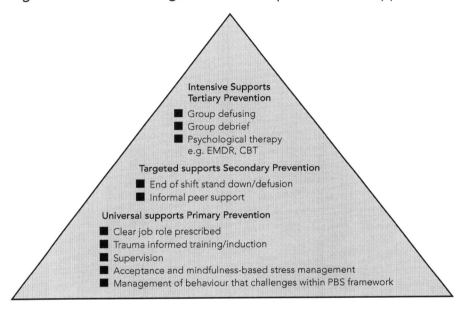

This training will also need to address helping staff to understand why people with intellectual disabilities may present behaviour that challenges. An understanding of the functional nature of the phenomena, at both a general and person-specific level, will help replace unhelpful beliefs that the staff member about why the person is doing what they are doing. Take Paula, who believed that John was being ungrateful and taking her for granted. This belief made the incident a personal attack on her. Perhaps the impact might have been different had she understood that John did not understand what was happening and was trying to escape from a situation he found aversive. He had no other way to express his anxiety and just wanted the personal care to stop. Understanding that this was not anything to do with Paula as a person, and that it was just about the situation, may well have reduced the emotional impact of the incident for her. This sort of understanding is derived from a functional behavioural assessment. Services need to develop this sort of understanding in their staff in regards to why the people they support might present behaviour that challenges (see Chapter 5).

Recruitment also needs to present a realistic picture of working with people who may present behaviour that challenges. Staff need to be prepared for the psychological impact of being involved in an incident. Researchers have recently begun to realise that staff can often be traumatised by an incident. This trauma can have an impact on the everyday functioning of the staff member, and informing people what they might experience will go some way to aid their recovery, along with practical tips delivered via staff training, including the importance of simple things such as exercise and utilising deep breathing. A focus on breathing is an integral part of 'acceptance and mindfulness-based stress management' and there is an emerging evidence base that introducing this to staff teams can have a positive impact on psychological well-being, and an indirect impact on the challenging behaviour presented by the people who use the service, for example Smith and Gore (2012).

Supervision

Regular supervision of staff provides an opportunity to build resilience. We have already stressed the importance of on the job support for staff. In addition to more typical discussion-based supervision, recent innovative ideas have sought to use video reflective practice as a way of developing staff competence, whereby the staff member videos themselves working with the person and looks back at the video with a practice leader using a series of prompts to reflect on the videoed interactions. One of the interesting side effects of this process has been the extent to which this appears to facilitate more positive interactions between the person and the member of staff (see Chapters 7 and 17).

Risk management

If we are identifying incidents of behaviour that challenges as a potential challenge to the psychological well-being of staff, it would appear to make a lot of sense to suggest that if we can reduce the chances of these incidents happening, then this would make a significant contribution to improving staff well-being. There is a requirement for good behaviour support based on an understanding of the functions of the behaviour. These plans should include a wide range of reactive strategies designed to make the behaviour less likely to occur, along with a range of reactive strategies designed to manage incidents in the most effective way, i.e. quickly and safely. So, if the likely occurrence of incidents is reduced, this would help, as would clear and effective strategies to manage any incidents quickly and safely, should they occur (see Chapter 10).

Targeted supports/secondary prevention

End of shift stand down

When staff have had a bad day, amid the chaos and confusion that can ensue it would be all too easy just to let them go home without recognition of what they had to face. This is a point where the response from the organisation is vital, and an opportunity for the worth of the staff member to be validated. It would be good practice at the end of each shift, and especially so if here had been an incident, for the shift leader to acknowledge the contribution made by each member of staff and to check on a very practical level that they are okay to go home. This is equivalent to the concept of 'stand down' in the emergency services, and would hopefully defuse any negative emotional impact of the incident. This practice, either conducted as an individual or group initiative, could also alert the organisation to the need for more focused intensive support where a staff member is particularly affected.

Social support

The research regarding what helps most with trauma universally, points to the importance of social support. People make the difference, thus services should be organised so that both informal and formal peer support is available. Formal peer support can be achieved through regular staff meetings. Informal support is more difficult to arrange by definition, but as a minimum, services should do all they can to make sure staff spend regular time with each other. Of particular concern would be services where staff work alone, so the provision of some regular time for these staff to spend with other staff is vital.

Intensive support/tertiary prevention

If a staff member has been involved in a particularly impactful incident, or exposed to multiple or ongoing incidents, they are likely to be in need of some sort of additional emotional support. The default position has been the provision of debriefing. Indeed, debriefing appears in most, if not all, practice guidance in relation to the management of behaviour that challenges incidents. When the purpose is stated, it is usually twofold: a) for the service to learn from the incident and b) to provide emotional support. To a large extent the first task is straightforward, the person is asked what happened, what went wrong, how it could be improved etc. The task of provision of emotional support is less straightforward, and practice leaders and managers would rarely be trained in how to provide effective emotional support. More often than not, they will try to do this at the same time as asking the staff member what they did wrong to cause the incident, or even more foolishly, think that by asking the staff members such questions this is akin to providing emotional support. In the case of Paula she did not find her debrief at all useful, as the main focus appeared to be on organisational learning. This is not at all uncommon, and if staff have been traumatised by the event, asking them to recall in detail what occurred runs the risk of traumatising them over again. In addition, the National Institute for Clinical Excellence (NICE) guidance on PTSD does not recommend single session individual debriefing as routine practice. The evidence used by NICE to come to this conclusion has been considered poor quality and is quite controversial (Rose et al, 2003). Nevertheless, it should be routine practice for a senior person to take a staff member who has been affected aside, in a sensitive manner, to check that they are okay, expressing concern for their welfare. However, given the pitfalls alluded to previously, specific training should be provided to staff members who are given this role.

The evidence base for group debriefing is more encouraging and, for exceptionally impactful services, should consider the provision of group debriefing as part of their range of staff supports. In addition, services should be aware of the extent to which each individual staff member has been affected, and have a clear strategy for signposting on to specialist psychological therapy if required.

Summary and conclusion

■ Staff who have good psychological well-being are essential for the provision of good positive behavioural support.

■ Dealing with incidents of behaviour that challenges can be emotionally impactful for staff.

■ The emotional impact is not solely determined by the incident, and a range of organisational and individual factors can affect the impact.

■ Services need to develop a multi-tiered approach to the support of the psychological well-being of staff.

■ This should include a range of both proactive and reactive strategies.

References

Hatton C, Emerson E, Rivers H, Mason H, Mason L, Swarbrick R, Kiernan C, Reeves D & Alborz A (1999) Factors associated with staff stress and work satisfaction in services for people with learning disability. *Journal of Learning Disability Research* **43** 253–267.

Rose S, Bisson J & Wessely S (2003). A systematic review of single-session psychological interventions ('debriefing') following trauma. *Psychotherapy and Psychosomatics* **72** (4) 176–184.

Smith M & Gore N (2012) Outcomes of a 'Train the Trainers' approach to an acceptance-based stress intervention in a specialist behaviour that challenges service. *International Journal of Positive Behavioural Support* **2** (1) 39–48.

Further reading

Baker P (2017) Attending to debriefing as post-incident support of care staff in intellectual disability behaviour that challenges services: an exploratory study. *International Journal of Positive Behavioural Support* **15** (1) 38–44.

Thompson L & Rose J (2011) Does organizational climate impact upon burnout in staff who work with people with intellectual disabilities? A systematic review of the literature. *Journal of Intellectual Disabilities* **15** (3) 177–193.

Chapter 17: Working together with families

By Isabelle Garnett & Holly Young

Summary

To support people with learning disabilities in a person-centred way support services should make use of the knowledge and understanding that their families have. There are barriers to working well with families, but these can be overcome with respect, good communication and by building trust. Family carers often have negative and even traumatic experiences of their family member's previous support. Support workers should bear in mind the difficulties family carers face and be flexible in working with them, as well as helping them get the support they need to continue in their vital caring role.

Why is this chapter important?

'Families are usually the main source of love, care and support for children and adults with learning disabilities... Even when people leave home, they do not leave the family. Families continue to offer a lifetime of involvement, support and advocacy.'
(Department of Health, 2009)

Family plays an important role in all our lives, but the role they play in the life of a person who has learning disability, autism or both is even more vital.

Families know and love their relative best. They have known them since birth and are usually a constant presence in their life. Consequently, families have a deep understanding of their relative's needs, strengths and hopes. For people who have complex needs or display behaviour that challenges, it is really important that their history is 'held', learnt from and used to provide effective support.

Working together with families will therefore increase your understanding of the person you support. This in turn makes your job easier and, most importantly, improves outcomes for the person you care for. This chapter explores why building good relationships with families is so vital and suggests positive ways in which you can do this.

What is important to understand about families?

There is no such thing as a 'typical family'

Most individuals have people in their lives that are described as 'family', though what constitutes a family varies greatly. There is a wide diversity of family situations and types, and individual circumstances differ enormously. Equally, the level of involvement of family in a person's life can vary considerably and change at different times.

Understanding each family context is therefore essential to offering appropriate support. Factors to reflect on include:

- variety of family members and their relation to the person
- where families live
- culture
- ages
- family roles
- differences in relationships and closeness
- the needs of family carers, such as learning disabilities, autism, mental health.

It is important to avoid making assumptions

Putting aside any preconceived ideas you may have and considering each family context, is crucial. For example, one of the most damaging misconceptions families frequently report is that their relative's learning disability, autism or both is somehow their fault. The reality is that anyone can have a child with learning disability, autism or both. It is no-one's fault.

Not all families are the same. Just because a family seems just like another that you have worked with, it doesn't mean they are. Try not to let any opinions you have formed about family carers get in the way of how you work with them.

Families can be powerful advocates

It is good practice to engage with family carers as partners. Families can be powerful advocates and they bring a unique and long-term perspective. They are highly motivated to speak up for their family member's rights. See later in this chapter for more on working together with families to increase the person's support package or access more services for them.

'I will always be a part of my son's life. I know I am important to him, even though he can't tell me that in words. I know that come what may, I can rely on my family to always be there for me – and it's even more important for him to have that too.'
(Family carer)

Families are long term

Adults with learning disabilities and behaviour described as challenging are likely to be supported by a range of paid workers who may be very important to the individual, but often only for a relatively short period in their lives. The continuity of family can therefore be particularly important.

People with learning disabilities whose behaviour is challenging to services are likely to be marginalised and disadvantaged. It is therefore even more important that strong family relationships are maintained and encouraged.

Families may have mixed experiences of support and services

'We wanted support and services that fitted around our son, not services that he had to fit into – because he couldn't fit into them!'
(Family carer)

'As parents we have to spend a lot of time fighting for our children.'
(Family carer)

'I have supported many families who have been failed time and again. Services may promise the world, but not provide the right support or neglect the individual. Years of battling for what their family member has a right to can have a lasting impact on families.'
(Family support worker)

Consider the family's journey up to this point. Many people with learning disabilities go through a series of failed placements or move around a lot. The family may have been let down or experienced conflicts with services. It is helpful if support workers recognise that the negative experiences families have had before can affect how they behave and communicate now. Think about:

■ Families being excluded from contact or decision making.

■ Legal battles on behalf of their family member.

■ Impact of austerity and cuts to services.

■ Traumatic experiences including abuse.

■ Particular pressures families face.

Families are under unique pressures

'I would like to be a parent to my disabled child and my other children rather than a doctor, nurse, social worker, fighter and carer.'
(Family carer)

Families of disabled people have identified many positive aspects of caring. However, there are a range of ways in which families can be disadvantaged. These include high levels of stress, financial disadvantage, adverse impact on the carers' health, feelings of isolation, poor housing and an increased rate of relationship breakdown. As one family carer describes:

'My son's neurodevelopmental paediatrician told me I was lucky my husband was still with me. I was taken aback and asked her why she had said that. She explained that very few of the parents on her caseload's marriages had survived.'

Families of individuals with learning disabilities whose behaviour is described as challenging are likely to be even more at risk of these disadvantages. There may be additional disadvantage for families from black and minority ethnic communities.

We also know that people with learning disabilities who access services are supported by a range of people who come and go from their lives. Families have to deal with the interactions between all this support and manage communications with everyone.

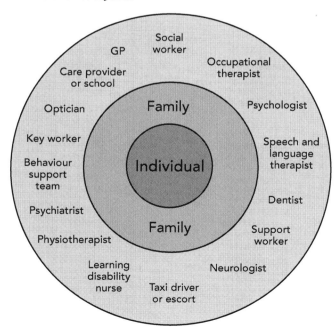

As one parent put it:

> 'I'm constantly writing letters, filling out forms, attending hospital appointments as well as all the day-to-day care she needs. It's definitely a full-time job.'

The most common difficulty of being a carer is isolation. Being socially isolated makes it harder to deal with stress and all too often this leads to mental health problems for family carers.

> 'It feels as if I have been thrown off a cliff into deep water and I don't know how to swim. All around me there are people who can help me or teach me to swim. But I can't get to them and they don't help me, and I know that eventually I will go under.'
> (Family carer)

> 'In relation to our own mental health, I think we have become used to living on the edge although we are aware that the stress is bound to take a toll.'
> (Family carer)

Barriers to working together

Several factors can get in the way of support workers working effectively with families, including:

- limited resources
- lack of appropriate local services
- busy jobs
- mistrust from families
- limited access to training
- the organisation's attitude towards family involvement.

> 'I fully understand the frustration families feel when dealing with professionals; our seeming inability to listen, our defensiveness at being challenged and our tedious obsession with our own systems comes across to families as a fundamental lack of humility and respect. Partnership working means being more person-centred and ultimately making better decisions but it also means professionals behaving better.'
> (Managing director of a support provider)

Scenario: Steven

Steven is a young adult with learning disabilities, who lives in a small care home. His parents take an active role in his support and understand his needs well. In the past they have experienced conflict with Steven's previous support provider, who did not share information with them and excluded them from decision making.

Steven is having problems sleeping so his parents speak to the team leader, Abby, about this when they visit. They ask how his sleep is being monitored and what information they can see. Abby explains that the team are keeping a record of when Steven gets up in the night and what he does when he wakes up. She offers to email them this record every week. However, there is a technical problem that week and Abby can't email the information. After a few days Steven's parents email her to ask for the sleep record. Abby replies two days later to say there is a problem and she'll send it as soon as she can. Three days after that, she emails two weeks' worth of sleep records.

Steven's parents are worried about how disrupted his sleep is, so call Abby to arrange a meeting. The time that she is available is not convenient for them, but they make arrangements to be able to attend.

Before the meeting Steven's parents visit him and are alarmed to see he has a large bruise on his arm. A support worker tells them he hardly slept the night before last and was shouting and throwing things around his room. They think he got the bruise then. Steven's parents are upset that they weren't called about the incident.

In the meeting Steven's parents are upset that they have not been kept informed. A lot of the meeting is taken up with discussing the communications of the last few weeks, before they are able to move on to discuss Steven's support.

Why were Steven's parents upset?

What could Abby have done differently?

Overcoming the barriers

Tips for getting past the barriers to working together are:

- honest and open communication
- understand and accept the challenges each other faces
- acknowledge each other's expertise
- share information
- consider the family's other commitments
- respect individual family differences
- include family carers/relatives in training
- keep communication channels open, even if you disagree
- avoid conflict.

What you can do to support family involvement

Start by stepping into their shoes

The importance of empathy cannot be overstated. In order to work together we need to understand one another, so understanding family carers and considering their situation is vital.

Take time to listen to families, get to know them and their perspective.

Respect family carers and their role

The opinions, expertise and experience of families should never be underestimated. Remember that their role is long term. Family carers are likely to hold far more information in their memories and experiences than can ever be written in a file!

Try not to make assumptions about the family carers you meet. Give them the benefit of the doubt.

> 'Sometimes family carers are described as "difficult" – but I have yet to meet a single one who is "difficult" for the sake of it. If a family carer is "difficult" there is a reason – it may have been something that has happened recently, or many years ago – but there is a reason, usually a very good one, why they are distrustful, and they need support and understanding to build a new relationship.'
> (Family support worker)

Families can contribute a lot:

- Years of knowledge and understanding of their family member.

- A full history of what support the person has or hadn't received in the past and how this has affected them.

- They are motivated to achieve the best support possible.

- Additional expertise – families are not 'just' carers, they have other skills, professions and knowledge that they are willing to use.

Build trust

An honest approach is essential to building trust. Sometimes there will be situations that cannot be changed or are beyond the control of the service provider – being honest about this helps everyone to understand what can be changed and what cannot, and to discuss this openly.

Give families confidence that you will do your best to give their family member good support. You can do this by being open about the support. Tell the truth about what is difficult and the things that are not going well, but also what is going right for their family member. Sometimes support teams forget to tell families about the positives and only report back about incidents of behaviour described as challenging. However, other teams may be reluctant to give families news that may worry or disappoint them, so only tell them about positives. Giving a balanced picture will allow families to understand the current situation and will ensure they are not surprised by a sudden change reported to them 'out of the blue'.

> 'From the outset, I said I wanted to be kept informed – if she is ill, if her behaviour deteriorates, if she doesn't get on with people, if something happens. I may be able to help, to shed some light on things and we can put our heads together to find solutions.'
> (Family carer)

Work together

Problem solving together can be a great way of working in partnership. If the person is displaying a new behaviour that is challenging, or if they are trying something new that may be difficult for them, then work with their family to come up with the best way of going about this. The outcome should be better by combining your skills as support workers and their expertise as family carers. Another good way of building your relationship with families would be to form a 'united front' to ask for more services from health and social care.

Involve family carers in decision making; for specific decisions when the person needs support to decide, or when a best interests decision is being made. Involving families in long term planning (e.g. person-centred planning) for the person enables them to have input in day-to-day choices, such as diet, clothes and activities.

Be 'person-centred' to the whole family

When services are flexible enough to fit in with family's needs, the family have the best chance of being fully involved. Family carers often have complicated lives, so they benefit from support services making things as easy as possible for them. Think about how arrangements can be made to suit the families you work with, such as meeting times and venues that are convenient for them. Ensure methods of communication suit the family.

Communicating with families

Communicating is not just delivering a message, it's about asking, listening and acting on what is heard. When supporting people who display behaviour that challenges, no one person has all the answers, so it's important for communication to be two-way.

Communication is important for:

- building trust
- working together
- finding solutions.

Scenario: communication

A parent regularly phones the service on weekdays when they get home from work. This is not long after the shift change in the service. The parent always asks about their daughter;

'How is she doing?'

Support worker: 'I don't know I've just come on shift.'

Parent: 'What has she done today?'

Support worker: 'I'm not sure, I wasn't here.'

Parent: Well do you know what she's having for dinner?'

Support worker: 'No, sorry I'm not on dinner duty tonight.'

How would this make you feel as a parent?

What can the support worker do to avoid this?

Good communication with families is:

- timely – don't delay
- honest – communicating bad and good news
- responding to family's priorities
- speaking plainly and avoiding jargon
- respectful tone and words.

Helping families get support

Families may need support, information and signposting for a range of issues that could arise:

- Decision making under the Mental Capacity Act (2005).
- Support to make complaints or access legal advice.
- Benefits, grants and other finances.
- Bereavement support.

- Emotional support and peer support.

- Taking their family member with learning disabilities on holiday.

- Finding an advocate to attend a meeting with them.

Use the area's Local Offer and directories (such as the Family Carers' Information Directory) to signpost families to support organisations and resources. Reliable information on a range of topics is available from Citizen's Advice Bureau at www.citizensadvice.org.uk, including a tool to write complaint letters. With a little research, a range of helplines, peer support groups and forums can be found for emotional support for families.

Benefits of working together

Support is best when it is planned and monitored by the support provider and family. Both contribute valuable insight and ideas to improve the person's quality of life.

> 'The best scenario for us as a family has been when professionals and us have sat down together as equals and tried to work out what's going on for my son, and nobody knows more than anybody else, but we work together to get the best outcome for my son.'
> (Family carer)

At the end of the day, the support provider and families need to work together, so should do so in as positive and fair way as possible. Focus on the benefits of the family input, rather than any difficulties in working with them. A good working relationship will reduce stress for everyone involved and let family carers sleep well at night knowing that their relative is safe and happy.

Conclusion

There is room for improvement in all support services and working better with families can help you to deliver better support. The Challenging Behaviour Foundation asked families to identify some 'top tips' for working with families as partners. These tips reflect the principles in this chapter:

- Find out the family's hopes and aspirations for the individual.

- Get off to a good start by making and maintaining early contact and agreeing how this will be done.

- Be clear, accurate, open and truthful.

- Keep language clear and simple so it cannot be misinterpreted.

- Take any concerns of the family seriously.

- Be an active and empathetic listener.
- Stay approachable and be contactable even if you disagree.
- Personalise written communication and never use generic statements about an individual.
- Use your creativity to seek out the individual's views when appropriate.
- Signpost families to sources of independent advice and support.

Families want the best possible care for their relative and are important allies in helping you to achieve this. A key point to remember is that most families want to work as partners. They want to be a positive influence in the life of their relative. Ultimately, families and service providers have the same fundamental aim: to enable the person to have a good quality of life that is rewarding and fulfilling.

Key learning point

Families should be equal partners in supporting people with learning disabilities. You can enable this by understanding their perspective, respecting their role and supporting them in a way that best suits them.

Reference

Department of Health (2009) *Valuing People Now Summary Report* [online]. Available at: https://assets.publishing.service.gov.uk/government/uploads/system/uploads/attachment_data/file/215891/dh_122387.pdf (accessed January 2019).

Further reading

State of Caring 2018 (Carers UK)
https://www.carersuk.org/news-and-campaigns/state-of-caring-survey-2018 (accessed January 2019).

Impact of Caring on Families (Challenging Behaviour Foundation)
www.challengingbehaviour.org.uk/being-family-carer/the-impact-of-caring (accessed January 2019).

Carers Matter – Everybody's Business (Skills for Care)
https://www.skillsforcare.org.uk/Document-library/Skills/Carers/Partthree.pdf (accessed January 2019).

BILD
http://www.bild.org.uk/our-services/books/good-support/partnership-working-with-family-carers/ (accessed January 2019).

Chapter 18: Working for change – policy and practice contexts

By Viv Cooper

Summary

This chapter will outline the background policies and best practice guidance that underpin current learning disability practice, and the challenges and opportunities they present to provide the right care, in the right place, at the right time for people with learning disabilities. It will begin by considering policies that apply to us all, moving on to those that are specifically about people with learning disabilities. The role of support providers and support workers is to put these policy principles into practice, delivering best practice as described in other chapters, with the aim of achieving good outcomes for people with learning disabilities who display behaviour described as challenging. Policy and best practice guidance can provide a real opportunity to drive change to improve the lives of people with learning disabilities who display behaviour described as challenging.

Introduction: what is policy?

We are all citizens of our society, which is governed by a range of legislation (laws that we live by, designed to protect us all (see Chapter 4)), and by government **policy**. A government policy is a document that sets out what the government will do and how it will do it.

> 'The term 'government policy' can be used to describe any course of action which intends to change a certain situation. Think of policies as a starting point for government to take a course of action that makes a real life change. Government uses policy to tackle a wide range of issues.'

We know that people with learning disabilities still experience inequalities and social injustice – policy can be used to drive action to change this.

The wealth of policies that exist can be divided into three categories when we consider how policy can drive change for people with learning disabilities:

1. There are numerous **generic policies** that apply to us all – for example, policies on transport, health, housing or climate change.

2. There are also policies that are **targeted at particular issues**, or at groups of individuals according to their shared characteristics, such as age or particular health issue, for example, children, older people, or people with mental health issues. These policies apply to everyone within that group. This means, for example, that a policy relating to older people will include older people with learning disabilities. The government has a number of policies for disabled people that set out how it aims to support all people who have a disability to reduce inequalities, and these policies apply to people with learning disabilities.

3. There are also a number of policies that apply specifically to **people with learning disabilities**. Some of these focus on practices and support around behaviour described as challenging.

A policy is usually developed in recognition that there is a need to have a particular focus on an issue of concern or on a group of people because they may be at risk of, or vulnerable to, disadvantage. The Equality Act (2010) (see Chapter 4) describes disability as a 'protected characteristic' and people with learning disabilities are within this group. People with learning disabilities who also display behaviour described as challenging have often been described as a disadvantaged group within a disadvantaged group, or 'doubly disadvantaged'– clear policy provides us with a framework to ensure we support them to access the same life opportunities as everyone else.

This chapter will outline the main polices that you need to be aware of in your work supporting people with learning disabilities who display behaviour described as challenging. We know from research that people with learning disabilities often experience:

■ poor health

■ exclusion from their local community and activities and services

■ unemployment.

We also know that people with learning disabilities are likely to be given psychotropic medication even though they do not have a diagnosed mental health condition. Those who display behaviour that challenges may be:

■ excluded from local support and services

■ placed long distances from their family homes

■ placed in 'assessment and treatment units' (ATUs) where they may stay for many years

■ subjected to physical restraint and seclusion (solitary confinement).

People with learning disabilities who display behaviour described as challenging have the same rights as everyone else, but are vulnerable to an increased risk of abuse, neglect and poor practice. Policy and best practice guidance are tools that can be used to challenge this and to drive change.

Key important generic policies

Some generic (i.e. for the general population) policies are particularly important for people with learning disabilities and those who care for them, including:

Health policy

■ We all want to live happy, fulfilled and interesting lives, and to do this good health (physical health and mental health) is key. We know however that people with learning disabilities die at a much younger age than the general population and that these premature deaths are often preventable. Public health policies promoting healthy lifestyles and the importance of good health are therefore important. Policies that promote regular health checks and screening, early intervention and prevention, healthy diets, mental well-being and regular exercise all apply to people with learning disabilities too.

Lifelong learning

■ This policy is based on the principle that our ability to learn exists throughout our whole lives and that learning improves our quality of life. Many of us continue our learning after leaving school or college – either through training for work, or for a particular interest or hobby. Many people with learning disabilities have their education disrupted, or are denied access to further education. People with learning disabilities who display behaviour described as challenging may be excluded from education opportunities because of the behaviours they display – because they don't 'fit in' or they are seen as disruptive, or it is not even considered as an option for them.

Employment policy

■ The government aims to have a high rate of employment but there are a number of groups where the rates remain low. Unemployment amongst disabled people is high and the government has set a target to increase the number of disabled people in employment by an extra one million between 2014 and 2020, believing their changes to the benefit system will help to incentivise this. The number of people with learning disabilities in employment remains low and there continue to be attempts to address this (see the *Valuing Employment Now* report (Department of Health, 2009a)).

Disability policy

- The government's Office for Disability Issues (ODI) 'supports the development of policies to remove inequality between disabled and non-disabled people'. The social model of disability focuses on addressing and overcoming the disabling attitudes and environments created by society, and removing barriers that restrict life choices and chances for disabled people. These policies apply to people with learning disabilities and provide the fundamental principles on which learning disability policy is based. They are focused on ensuring that people with disabilities have the same life opportunities as everyone else and that reasonable adjustments are made to make this happen, with access to specialist support and input if it is needed.

Within these policies there are common commitments to ways of working to drive change:

- **Prevention and early intervention** (it is best to prevent a problem from happening in the first place – but if a problem does arise, do something early before it becomes a big problem).

- **Personalisation** (support and services should be 'person centred' – i.e. they should be flexible and adaptable and designed around the person, rather than expecting the person to 'fit in' to what is available).

- **Partnership working** (working together).

- **Value for money** (the resources available should be used well and to best effect).

Learning disability policy

Learning disability policy over the years reflects the move from sending people away from their homes and families to live in large institutions long stay hospitals, to a community care model of support and services. The following policies are current and are those which are most relevant to your work.

The Mansell Report (1993)

This guidance report from the Department of Health set out how local areas should organise support and services to meet the needs of individuals with learning disabilities who display behaviour described as challenging. *The Mansell Report* is an important report – its recommendations and principles remain current despite that it was published in 1993.

The key principles within the report are the need to develop local services to support people with learning disabilities whose behaviour was described as challenging. A key recommendation was:

'*Commissioners should invest in two aims:*

■ *To develop and expand capacity of local services for people with learning disabilities to understand and respond to challenging behaviour.*

■ *To provide specialist services locally which can support good mainstream practices as well as directly serve a small number of people with the most challenging needs.*'

(Department of Health, 1993, p. 28)

Valuing People: A new strategy for learning disability in the 21st century (2001)

This was the first learning disability policy published by the government for nearly 30 years and was very significant. It focused on better chances for people with learning disabilities and set out four overarching principles on which support and services for people with learning disabilities should be based: rights, choice, independence and inclusion. It identified the need to support carers, to improve health outcomes for people, to address the lack of housing and housing options, to enable people to lead fulfilling lives and to access employment as well as raising the quality of services. *Valuing People* (Department of Health, 2001) acknowledged that people with learning disabilities were often marginalised and disadvantaged in our society, and that there was a need for a national strategy to change this.

Importantly, the policy included details of how the changes would be made and it introduced a requirement for each local authority to set up a learning disability partnership board to oversee the delivery of the changes that were needed and make sure that the needs of people with learning disabilities were considered in every aspect of their local community. The board would be made up of senior people from social care, education and health and importantly, people with learning disabilities and family carers. A team of advisors was set up for advice and support, people with learning disability knowledge and skills (national and regional), and there was ring-fenced money to drive the change forward.

Valuing People raised the profile of people with learning disabilities – it made sure that attention was focused on them. For the first time it provided people with learning disabilities and their families with specific opportunities to be involved at a strategic level in planning support and services in their local area – and to challenge if they were not.

Revised Mansell Report (2007) and Raising our Sights (2010)

Although *Valuing People* had a positive impact on the lives of many people with learning disabilities and their families, it became clear that less attention and progress was being made for people with complex needs. Professor Mansell was commissioned by the Department of Health to write two reports: one about people with profound and multiple disabilities (*Raising our Sights*, Mansell, 2010) and a follow up (Department of Health, 2007) to his 1993 report about people with learning disabilities who display behaviour described as challenging. Re-stating the recommendations in his 1993 report, Mansell stated that we should:

> '… stop using services which are too large to provide individualised support; serve people too far from their homes; and do not provide people with a good quality life in the home or as part of the local community, in favour of developing more individualised, local solutions which provide a good quality of life.'

Valuing People Now: A new three-year strategy for people with learning disabilities (2009b)

In 2009, the Valuing People policy was 'refreshed' and *Valuing People Now* (Department of Health, 2009b) was published. It also acknowledged that more needed to be done to improve the lives of people with complex needs. This policy focused on four key areas: including everyone, personalisation, having a life (health, housing, work and education and relationships) and people as citizens (advocacy, transport, leisure and social activities, being safe and access to justice).

Valuing Employment Now: Real jobs for people with learning disabilities (2009a)

As employment opportunities for people with learning disabilities was an area where there had been little change, a dedicated cross-government policy was published in 2009 (Department of Health, 2009a):

> 'We need a dedicated employment strategy for people with learning disabilities because they have not benefited from the progress made for disabled people generally. While the employment rate of disabled people in Britain overall has risen steadily, that of people with learning disabilities is much lower… this represents a waste of talent and opportunity for people with learning disabilities, employers and our wider economy and society.'

Transforming Care (2012)

Sadly it is often the case that policy and guidance is issued after a major scandal. In 2011, BBC Panorama exposed significant abuse of people with learning disabilities in a private hospital called Winterbourne View in a programme called 'Undercover Care'. This scandal led to a review of how people ended up in places like Winterbourne View. The review concluded that there was a need to change many parts of the system; to transform how people with learning disabilities and/ or mental health problems and/or autism who display behaviour described as challenging are supported. The Transforming Care Programme set out targets to reduce the number of people with learning disabilities and/or autism who are stuck in inpatient units (often for a long time, and far from their home areas) by developing better community support and services. Each local area has a Transforming Care Partnership which leads this work, but the programme has been strongly criticised as it has not 'transformed care'.

Positive and Proactive Care: Reducing the need for restrictive interventions (2014)

This policy was developed as a direct result of the Winterbourne View abuse scandal, to address the high rates of restrictive practices (e.g. physical restraint, seclusion and segregation) which are over-used as a response to behaviour that challenges (Department of Health, 2014).

It aimed to:

> ' ... provide a framework to support the development of service cultures and ways of delivering care and support which better meet people's needs and which enhance their quality of life. It provides guidance on the delivery of services together with key actions that will ensure that people's quality of life is enhanced and that their needs are better met, which will reduce the need for restrictive interventions and promote recovery.'

Building the Right Support (2015)

The failure of the Transforming Care programme to deliver its objectives led to the development of *Building the Right Support* (NHS England, 2015). This is the plan to deliver the change required and has two main strands – to close inpatient beds for people with learning disabilities, and to build more community support (to stop people ending up in hospital, and also to enable those that are in hospital to move out).

Putting it into practice

So what does all this policy and guidance mean for people with learning disabilities whose behaviour is described as challenging? The range and scope of the policies are an indication of the progress that is yet to be made to ensure that people with learning disabilities enjoy the same life opportunities as everyone else. The multi-stakeholder Challenging Behaviour National Strategy Group (CB NSG): (https://www.challengingbehaviour.org.uk/driving-change/driving-change. html) worked together to develop a charter which sets out all the things that need to be in place to get the right support in the right place at the right time.

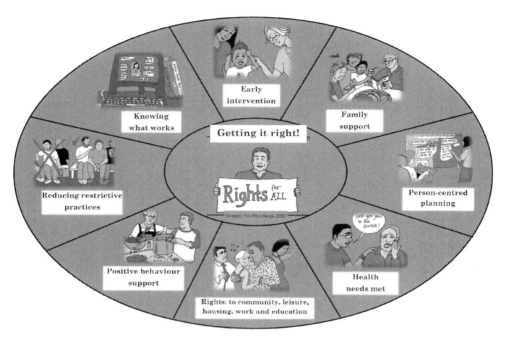

Adapted from the CB NSG charter. Graphic by @MendoncaPen
www.penmendonca.com

Using policy to drive change

Policy provides us with a framework to improve how people with learning disabilities are supported in two main ways:

1. As the basis for new ways of working in line with the policy principles.

2. To challenge when practice is not in line with policy.

The policies outlined previously have led to a range of best practice guidance, frameworks and initiatives and have great potential for improving the lives of people with learning disabilities whose behaviour is described as challenging.

A **personalisation** approach works well for people with complex needs, and can be used to deliver policy and tailor individualised support around a person.

Personalisation is defined broadly by central government as 'the way in which services are tailored to the needs and preferences of citizens. The overall vision is that the state should empower citizens to shape their own lives and the services they receive.'

(HM Government Policy Review, 2007, p. 7)

Previously, the approach was to group people together around their support needs, and therefore there were 'specialist challenging behaviour' houses where the only thing the people living there had in common was their behaviour. People with learning disabilities were expected to 'fit in' to services that would take them, regardless of how far away from their local area the services were, and there was little attention on what was important to the person and what their outcomes were. The policy emphasis on rights, choice, independence and inclusion has challenged this approach and support and services must adopt an individualised approach to meeting a person's needs. It has meant greater emphasis on how the support and services deliver a better quality of life for the person – an 'outcome-focused' approach.

Case study: policy into practice

Robert is a young man in his early twenties. He is very active, enjoys being outdoors and going for long walks, as well as playing football. He likes routine and being supported by people who can communicate with him through signing, and who are also lively and active. He displays a range of behaviours described as challenging, and moved from an out of area residential school back to his home area to a residential care home, which he shares with four other people who he did not know previously. The five residents have very different needs, including some with mobility and sensory needs, but what they have in common is that they all display behaviours that are challenging, although these behaviours take different forms. Robert's family are pleased that he is now more local, but are concerned that he is learning new behaviours from the people he now shares with. He shows no interest in being with his fellow residents, and actively seeks to be in a different part of the house from them when he is at home. The service has one minibus for trips out, and so for any outing at least two residents go together, and sometimes they all go. Robert and one of the residents 'wind each other up', so this has to be very carefully managed. Due to the level of need of all the residents, many support staff are in the home too, and there is much 'coming and going' of staff which means Robert is supported by many different people, some of whom do not know him well and cannot sign.

At Robert's review his family suggest that he would prefer to live alone with his own staff team to support him. They point to government policy and to *Valuing People* that describes supported living, to personalised approaches and to *Building the Right Support* and a service model that says that people with learning disabilities have the right to choose who they live with. Although Robert is non-verbal he is clearly demonstrating through his behaviour that he does not want to share his home with other people.

Robert's needs are reviewed – there is clear evidence of his preferences, and evidence that his behaviours are increasing posing a risk to himself and to others. Working together, his family, keyworker, care manager and support provider draw up a specification for a new supported living service for Robert. It takes a long time, and requires a great deal of work and co-ordination, but eventually Robert moves into his own bungalow, rented from a housing association and adapted to meet his specific needs.

Robert continues to have high support needs, but he is much happier, and the risks and behaviours that came from sharing with others have been eliminated. →

> His support is much more person-centred, he can participate in activities he
> enjoys, and has his own regular staff support team who can communicate with him
> and who he enjoys being supported by. His family and his support provider work
> together to make sure that new opportunities and activities are explored and that
> his support is designed to focus on delivering good outcomes for Robert.

The publication of policies has led to a series of practice guidance that helps
us to translate the policy into action. Whilst some policy initiatives have
a time limited delivery team or plan (with or without resources) there is
usually a need to have guidance about how to make the change happen.
In learning disability, there are some important initiatives that have been
developed, including:

National Institute for Health and Care Excellence (NICE) guidance

There are two NICE guides with a specific focus on behaviour that challenges.
These are the clinical guidelines on behaviour that challenges (2015), and the
service models guidelines (2018). The clinical guidance sets out how the needs
of an individual should be assessed and met, and the service guideline sets
out what services should be available locally. Commissioners and providers
are meant to use NICE guidelines to inform their work. Recommendations,
especially in the service model guidelines, are closely aligned to Mansell report
recommendations, and provide a real opportunity to use the recommendations
and implementation of the guidance to influence change.

Positive behaviour support (see Chapter 3)

When policy is implemented and best practice guidance is issued, the 'tools'
that are recommended should be evidence based (i.e. tried and tested and
shown to be effective). Positive behaviour support (PBS) is an evidence-
based framework for supporting people who display behaviour described as
challenging. A group of academics, clinicians and families worked together to
form a PBS academy: http://www.pbsacademy.org.uk, an informal collaboration
which has produced a range of tools and resources that are available to help
support providers and families deliver PBS.

STOMP

Alongside promoting and sharing good practice to deliver policy, there are
initiatives that are working to target and reduce poor practice. STOMP
stands for STopping Over Medication of People with a learning disability,
autism or both with psychotropic medication. It is a national project
involving many different organisations which are helping to stop the over
use of these medicines. Psychotropic medicines affect how the brain works
and include medication for psychosis, depression, anxiety, sleep problems and

epilepsy. Sometimes they are also given to people because their behaviour is seen as challenging and they act as a sedative.

People with a learning disability, autism or both, are more likely to be given these medicines than other people. Public Health England says that every day about 30,000 to 35,000 adults with a learning disability are taking psychotropic medicines, when they do not have the health conditions the medicines are for. Psychotropic medicines can cause problems if people take them for too long, take too high a dose or take them for the wrong reason. They also often have side effects which can affect the person's physical health and quality of life. The STOMP programme is focused on reviewing people's medication and reducing it if it is not required.

An overarching guide to put policy into practice are the guidelines *Challenging Behaviour: A unified approach* (Royal College of Psychiatrists & British Psychological Society, 2016). This guidance was developed across a range of professions (e.g. psychology, psychiatry, speech and language therapists, learning disability nursing), and promotes the partnership working model. This model sets out that a range of people and professions have roles to play in supporting people who display behaviour described as challenging, and that working together is most likely to deliver better outcomes for the person.

Key point

Policy and best practice guidance are important; they provide a framework for driving positive change for people with learning disabilities and should be used to improve how people are supported day-to-day.

Questions

- If you swapped places with the person/people you support would you feel well supported, happy and empowered? What would be important? What one change would make a positive difference?

- What action will you take to make the support you provide more person-centred?

- How will you use policy on health, employment and lifelong learning to improve the lives of the people you support?

- Does the service provider you work for use policy to deliver good practice? Can you suggest how to improve?

- How can you help the person you support to make more choices every day?

- What activity does the person you support really enjoy? How can you help them do it more often?

References

Challenging Behaviour National Strategy Group (2013) *The Challenging Behaviour Charter* [online]. Available at: https://www.challengingbehaviour.org.uk/learning-disability-files/CBF-Charter-2013.pdf (accessed February 2019).

Department of Health (1993) *Services for People with Learning Disabilities and Challenging Behaviour or Mental Health Needs* (The Mansell Report).

Department of Health (2001) *Valuing People: A new strategy for learning disability for the 21st century* [online]. Available at: https://assets.publishing.service.gov.uk/government/uploads/system/uploads/attachment_data/file/250877/5086.pdf (accessed February 2019).

Department of Health (2007) *Services for People with Learning Disabilities and Challenging Behaviour or Mental Health Needs* (The Mansell Report) (revised edition) [online]. Available at: https://www.kent.ac.uk/tizard/research/research_projects/dh2007mansellreport.pdf (accessed February 2019).

Department of Health (2009a) *Valuing Employment Now: Real jobs for people with learning disabilities* [online]. Available at: https://www.legislation.gov.uk/ukia/2009/179/pdfs/ukia_20090179_en.pdf (accessed February 2019).

Department of Health (2009b) *Valuing People Now: A new three-year strategy for people with learning disabilities* [online]. Available at: https://webarchive.nationalarchives.gov.uk/20130105064234/http:/www.dh.gov.uk/prod_consum_dh/groups/dh_digitalassets/documents/digitalasset/dh_093375.pdf (accessed February 2018).

Department of Health (2014) *Positive and Proactive Care: Reducing the need for restrictive interventions* [online]. Available at: https://assets.publishing.service.gov.uk/government/uploads/system/uploads/attachment_data/file/300293/JRA_DoH_Guidance_on_RP_web_accessible.pdf (accessed February 2019).

HM Government Policy Review (2007) *Building on Progress: Public services.* London: Prime Minister's Strategy Unit.

Mansell J (2010) *Raising our Sights: Services for adults with profound intellectual and multiple disabilities* [online]. Available at: https://www.mencap.org.uk/sites/default/files/2016-06/Raising_our_Sights_report.pdf (accessed February 2019).

NICE (2015) *Challenging Behaviour and Learning Disabilities: Prevention and interventions for people with learning disabilities whose behaviour challenges* [online]. Available at: https://www.nice.org.uk/guidance/ng11 (accessed February 2019).

NICE (2018) *Learning Disabilities and Behaviour that Challenges: Service design and delivery* [online]. Available at: https://www.nice.org.uk/guidance/ng93 (accessed February 2019).

NHS England (2015) *Building the Right Support* [online]. Available at: https://www.england.nhs.uk/wp-content/uploads/2015/10/ld-nat-imp-plan-oct15.pdf (accessed February 2019).

Royal College of Psychiatrists and British Psychological Society (2016) *Challenging Behaviour: A unified approach – update* [online]. Available at: https://www.bps.org.uk/sites/bps.org.uk/files/Policy/Policy%20-%20Files/Challenging%20behaviour-%20a%20unified%20approach%20%28update%29.pdf (accessed February 2019).

Chapter 19: Afterword: knowing where we are heading by knowing where we have been

By Tony Osgood & Peter Baker

Professor Jim Mansell (1952-2012) was fond of reminding his colleagues and students that, to paraphrase the philosopher George Santayana, those who fail to learn from history are likely to repeat its errors. In the UK we have much evidence that innovations and new policies relating to intellectual disability support, fundamentally rely on ordinary people to implement everyday best practice, and that what we know works is often hard to put into action by anyone other than those who support individuals daily.

In 2001, *Valuing People,* the government white paper concerning how to provide best support to people with intellectual disabilities, recommended the adoption of person-centred plans in order to begin building services and support around the person. In 2019, good person-centred plans are rarely found. People spend a good deal of time talking about being person-centred and yet we see the growth of private hospitals and assessment units across the UK, few of which can legitimately claim to be person-centred. It is almost as if the hard-learned lessons from abuse scandals of the 1960s, 1970s, 1980s and since, have been forgotten by those purchasing such provision, and those offering such provision. When a monetary value is given to people requiring support, too often the values we espouse walk when the money talks. Positive behavioural support (PBS) cannot limit itself to behaviour, because the central tenet of it is delivering quality of life *regardless* of behaviour that challenges. Behaviour that challenges is not a barrier but a call for better support, and PBS is for those who are passionate about changing for the better the experiences of people receiving services, the staff supporting them, and families advocating for the best practice for those they love. PBS is not for the faint-hearted.

In such a climate PBS has been heralded and introduced widely. What is often said to be PBS is no such thing, but is rather a relabelling of old ways of working. This means unless we have a clear definition of what good PBS looks like, it will be easy to claim anything is PBS: doing so will discredit PBS in much the same way as person-centred planning has been discredited. This makes the work of the PBS Academy so important. The academy provides clear definitions of what PBS *should* look like – namely, people leading active and enviable lives of high quality, where behaviour that challenges is not a barrier to community, relationships, and control of their own lives.

PBS is more than completing an assessment, and far more than implementing a mosaic of support strategies that amend or avoid predictors of behaviour that challenges, teach alternatives to behaviour that challenges, and resolve conflicts with some dignity in a way that can mend ruptured relationships. PBS is an approach to deliver a good quality of life. If an approach does not explicitly improve the lived experience of people it aims to support and enable, then it really is not PBS, no matter what it claims.

As it moves forward, PBS cannot afford to forget its own past, and the lessons to be learned. PBS cannot afford to turn a blind eye to quality of life in its pursuit of reliable data, and it must stick to its values as well as its graphs. It must be clear it is a blend of values and science, and be willing to speak up when it encounters poor practice.

We hope that this book begins your journey to think creatively, act in a person-centred manner, support in an evidence-based way, and enjoy your time working creatively with some of the most remarkable humans you will ever be likely to meet.